KNIT ME, DRESS ME, LOVE ME

Sue Stratford

DEDICATION

This book is dedicated to Ella Stratford.
Thank you for being such a fantastic
mother-in-law and grandma to our
little peskies.

KNIT ME, DRESS ME, LOVE ME

Sue Stratford

SEARCH PRESS

ACKNOWLEDGEMENTS

What a great experience making this book has been, partly because of all the fabulous people who have helped me along the way. Thank you to my marvellous editor, May Corfield, and to Carol Ibbetson for her tech-editing skill. I have to thank Phyl Christmas, who spent HOURS knitting every little item in this book to make sure I had not lost the plot while writing the patterns. Also grateful thanks to Maggie from The Textile Garden for rooting through her buttons and sending me such a fantastic selection. Thanks also to Nicole at CloudCraft – your felt is so great to work with! And last, but by no means least, thank you to everyone at The Knitting Hut, especially Heather, who has put up with me and my mad ideas. Don't worry Heather, there are plenty more mad ideas to come!

First published in 2017

Search Press Limited
Wellwood, North Farm Road,
Tunbridge Wells, Kent TN2 3DR

Text copyright © Sue Stratford 2017

Photographs by Paul Bricknell at Search Press Studios

Photograph on page 8 by Sue Stratford

Photographs and design copyright © Search Press Ltd 2017

ISBN: 978-1-78221-379-6

The Publishers and author can accept no responsibility for any consequences arising from the information, advice or instructions given in this publication.

Suppliers

If you have difficulty in obtaining any of the materials and equipment mentioned in this book, then please visit the Search Press website for details of suppliers:
www.searchpress.com

You are invited to view the author's work at:

www.suestratford.co.uk
Knittinghutsue on Ravelry
Sue Stratford Knits on Facebook
Knittinghutsue on Instagram
Knittinghutsue on Twitter

Printed in China

CONTENTS

Introduction 8

Materials and tools 10

Techniques 12

Decorative stitches 21

KNIT ME! 24

Tension (gauge) 26

DRESS ME! 56

LOVE ME!

INTRODUCTION

You know what us crafters are like... we love to build up a stash.

This book is the result of a yarn stash. A few years ago I bought some yarn, fabric and felt with the idea of making knitted bunnies in clothes for my daughters and their cousins for Easter. Years later, just before Easter, I remembered the long-forgotten yarn and cast on. By Easter Sunday I had five bunnies wearing little sewn dresses and shoes. I then came up with the idea of a mini version of each animal to use up the leftover yarn. The bunnies and their 'mini-me' playmates were well received and I was asked by friends for a pattern. They were so cute that I thought they deserved a whole wardrobe. So the original bunny has ended up with several friends and enough outfits to take them anywhere!

This is the idea behind the book. I have included seven adorable animals – a bunny, mouse, monkey, kitten, puppy, panda and teddy bear – each with a 'mini-me' companion and a wardrobe full of clothes. As well as the full knitted wardrobe for your new little friend, there are also some sewn clothes, complete with step-by-step instructions and photographs to accompany these. All the animals are the same size – 20.5cm (8in) tall – and so all the clothes, knitted or sewn, will fit whichever animal you decide to knit. Whether your animal is going to school, to a picnic, out in the snow, to the beach or even to bed, there are clothes to fit the occasion. There is even a set of underwear to maintain your toy's dignity! Each animal's mini-me – its very own 'toy' that is a simpler version of the big animals – is just 8.5cm ($3^3/_8$in) tall. My youngest daughter was fascinated by this and loves popping them in the baby carrier, the

sleeping bag or the Moses basket. All the accessories are given on pages 132–137.

All the animals are made using aran (10-ply/worsted) weight yarn so they are quick and easy to make; follow the measurements on pages 26 and 27 when sewing them together to make sure that the clothes will fit. It is very easy to over-stuff the animals, so keep measuring until you sew that final seam closed!

The knitted clothes are made using 4-ply (fingering) yarn, which enabled me to achieve the level of detail I wanted to make them look extra special. Scraps of yarn left over from other projects are ideal to use up – just check the pattern for quantities.

The sewn clothes are made mainly using clothes that my children had when they were small. The girl's pyjamas are made from my daughter's baby vest and the boy's star pyjamas from those worn by my son when he was only two (see both on page 119) – he is now eighteen! The photograph above shows my daughter wearing a yellow gingham school dress that I cut up and re-used to make the mouse's dress on page 71. Before cutting up the clothes I checked for any lace or fastenings on them that I could re-use; the buttons were really useful because, as they are baby and toddler clothes, they are tiny and so work well for these mini clothes. I love the idea of upcycling my children's old clothes into something they can play with and that I can

see every day, instead of them being hidden away in the loft. If you don't have old clothes to cut up, use any scraps of fabric that you have. I bought fat quarters of fabric that caught my eye – in fact, the frog fabric used for the shorts (page 89) was one of those impulse buys! I used my sewing machine to make the clothes, but you can sew them by hand if you prefer. Just be careful with your fabric choice, and select something that doesn't fray easily.

Have fun and happy crafting!

MATERIALS AND TOOLS

Yarn

I love to use unusual yarns in my designs but I know that sometimes these can be hard to get hold of or, worse, are discontinued. In this book the animals are all made using textured yarns, so if you can't find the exact yarn they will not be hard to replace. All the animals are knitted in aran (10-ply/worsted) weight yarn and for most of them you can knit the animal and its mini-me from one ball.

All the clothes are made using 4-ply (fingering) yarn so that I could get the level of detail in the garments. They are certainly quick to make and with a couple of balls of yarn you can make quite a selection of clothes. The amounts of yarn required are noted on each pattern. Virtually all balls of yarn have their weight and length on the ball band so it's not hard to calculate how much you will need.

For some of the accessories such as the Moses basket (page 134) and beach bag (page 85), I used double knitting (8-ply/light worsted) yarn. Again, one ball will go a long way with these little projects!

Toy stuffing

I always use a polyester toy stuffing that meets current toy safety standards. It is easy to use, fluffs up nicely and can also be washed without 'matting'.

Knitting needles

For the animals I have used 3.75mm (UK 9, US 5) knitting needles. These are smaller than you would usually use with this weight of yarn and so give a tighter finish, so that the toy stuffing does not show through the knitting.

However, it is worth making a quick tension swatch (see page 26) before you begin, to make sure the animals come out the right size. If they are too big, the sewn clothes won't fit.

As these are all small projects I like to use short, double-pointed knitting needles. These are also useful when it comes to the i-cord technique (see page 33 under *Ear edging*), which I have used for the mini-me arms and parts of the knitted clothes.

Sewing machine

The sewn clothes can be sewn by hand, particularly the felt dress on page 101. However, you will find it much quicker to use a sewing machine. As the clothes are small I used relatively small stitch settings on my machine. For the straight stitch I set the stitch length at 2.0. For the zigzag the width was set at 3.5 and the length 1.0. These can be used as a guide as not all sewing machines have the same settings.

Other materials

The clothes in this book are a great way to use up old buttons. You only need two or three for each project so dig deep in that button box for some old favourites! I have re-used buttons from some of the clothes I have cut up and used them on both the knitted and sewn clothes. A few unusual trimmings are also useful; again, some of these can be recycled. The girl's shortie pyjamas feature a small amount of trimming I bought to match the fabric.

I also used some embroidery threads to embroider on a few of the clothes, such as the dressing gown and the slippers (page 120 and 121).

I have used black beads for the animals' eyes, which gives them a real sense of character, but if the animal you make is a gift for a young child, do not use beads; use safety eyes instead or, alternatively, embroider the eyes on using French knots (see page 21).

TECHNIQUES

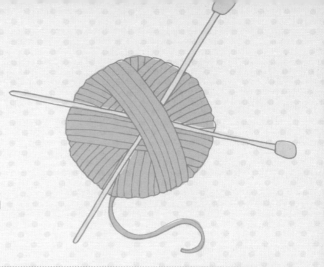

 ## Make one stitch (M1)

This easy technique creates an almost invisible increase and I use it on all my knitting projects. I first came across it in a sock pattern and from then onwards it has been my favourite way of increasing.

Increasing on a knit row

1 With the working yarn at the back of the work and holding the yarn in your left hand, make a loop, with the working yarn at the front of the loop.

2 Slide this loop onto your needle.

3 Tighten this new 'stitch', then knit to the end of the row.

4 On the following row, purl this stitch through the back of the loop to tighten it.

5 The finished increase looks like this.

Increasing on a purl row

1 With the working yarn at the front of the work and holding the yarn in your left hand, make a loop, with the working yarn at the front of the loop.

2 Slide this loop onto your needle and tighten. Purl to the end of the row.

3 On the following row, knit this stitch as normal.

4 The finished increase looks like this.

Wrap and turn (w&t)

Short row shaping is invaluable when creating a three-dimensional shape. Using this method you can turn round, mid-row, without leaving a hole in your work. When you first turn it does look like there will be a gap, but by the time you have worked back it disappears.

On a knit row

1 Knit to the stitch where you will turn and bring the yarn to the front of the work.

2 Slide the next stitch, without twisting it, from the left needle to the right needle.

3 Take the yarn around the stitch to the back of the work.

4 Slide the stitch, purlwise, back to the left-hand needle.

5 Turn your work. The wrapped stitch is now on the right-hand needle.

6 Purl back across the row.

7 When you come back to the wrapped stitch on the following knit row knit the wrap and the stitch together as follows:

8 Slide the stitch to the right-hand needle and, using the point of the left-hand needle, pick up the wrap of yarn around it.

9 Slide the stitch back from the right-hand to the left-hand needle.

10 Knit the wrap and the stitch together.

Wrap and turn on a purl row

1 Purl to the stitch where you will turn and take the yarn to the back of the work.

2 Slide the next stitch, purlwise, from the left-hand needle to the right-hand needle.

3 Take the yarn around the stitch to the front of the work.

4 Slide the stitch, purlwise, back to the left-hand needle.

5 Turn your work. The wrapped stitch is now on the right-hand needle. Knit back across the row.

6 When you come back to the wrapped stitch on the following purl row, purl the wrap and the stitch together as follows:

7 Slide the stitch to the right-hand needle and, using the point of the left-hand needle, pick up the wrap of yarn around it.

8 Slide the stitch back from the right-hand to the left-hand needle.

9 Purl the wrap and the stitch together.

Three-needle cast-off

This is a really neat way of casting off to save sewing a seam!
This technique is used for the animals' feet and the socks.

1 Divide the remaining stitches evenly between two needles and place with RS together.

2 Using a third needle, slide the needle through the first stitch on each needle.

3 Knit these two stitches together so that you have one stitch on the right-hand needle.

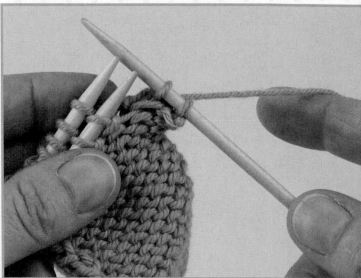

4 Knit the next stitch from each needle together, so that you have two stitches on the right-hand needle.

18

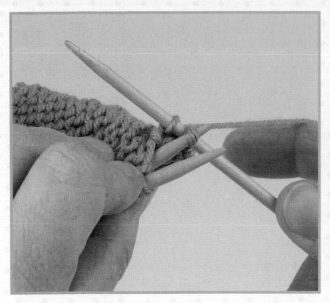

5 Cast off the first stitch in the usual way, by lifting it over the second stitch.

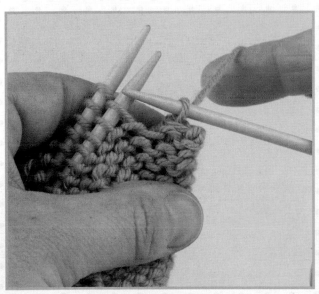

6 You now have one stitch on the right-hand needle.

7 Repeat steps 4 to 5 until you have one stitch remaining on the right-hand needle. Thread the yarn through the stitch to secure, and fasten off.

8 Turn to the right side.

Mattress stitch

This is a really neat way to sew your work together. You work with the right side facing you at all times and it gives you a lovely invisible seam. I have used a contrasting yarn colour so that you can see each step clearly.

1 Secure the yarn at the back of your work and bring the needle up through to the front, one stitch in from the edge.

2 Take the needle and yarn to the other side and slide through the 'bar' between the first and second stitch directly opposite the first stitch.

3 Pull the yarn slightly and slide the needle and yarn through the next 'bar' on the opposite side.

4 Continue in this way for a few stitches so that you have a 'ladder' line of stitches without tightening the yarn each time.

5 Hold the work firmly, pull the yarn and you will see the two rows of stitches join and the ladder will disappear.

The stitches are invisible on the finished seam.

6 Repeat these steps along the length of the row. Secure the yarn at the end of the seam.

DECORATIVE STITCHES

These stitches are used throughout the book to decorate many of the projects, knitted and sewn.

French knot

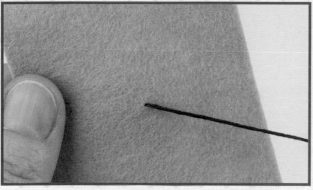

1 Secure the yarn on the reverse side and bring the sewing needle and yarn through to the front of the work.

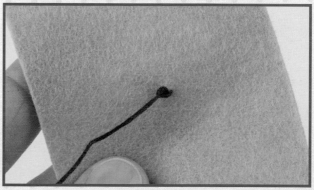

2 Thread the needle through the felt as shown.

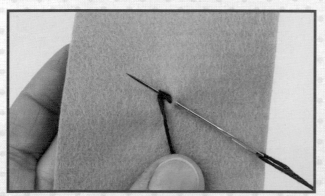

3 Wind the yarn around the needle twice, holding the working yarn tightly with your thumb to stop the stitch working loose.

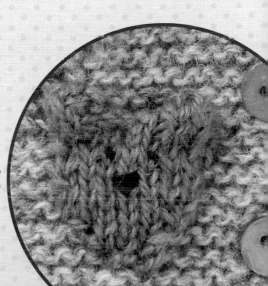

4 Pull the needle upwards to create a 'knot'.

5 Thread the needle back through to the reverse. The loops of yarn you made will now form a knot. Fasten off the yarn securely.

French knots are used for the eyes and nose on the bear-shaped pockets of the knitted coat (see page 106).

Chain stitch

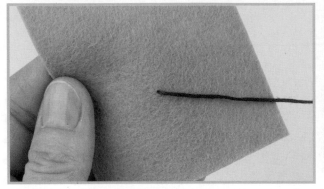 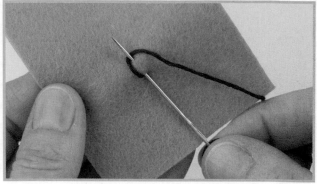

1 Start by bringing your threaded needle from the back of the work to the front.

2 Reinsert the needle from the front to the back next to where the needle came up, forming a loop, and bring the needle back through to the front of the work, so that the needle is inside the loop of thread.

 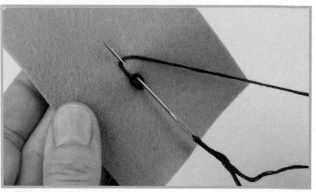

3 Pull the needle through to form the first chain.

4 Repeat steps 2 to 3 to create more stitches.

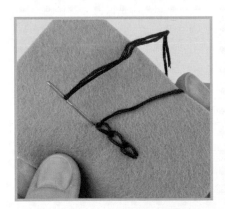 

Chain stitch details on the boys' Y-fronts (see page 122).

5 When you have as many stitches as you need, thread the needle to the back of the work, looping the yarn over the final stitch. Secure it on the back of the work.

Lazy daisy stitch

A lazy daisy stitch is formed using chain stitches. Work as for chain stitch (opposite); with lazy daisy stitch each stitch starts at the centre of the flower.

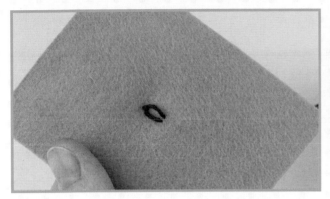

1 Make a chain stitch as shown in steps 1–3 on page 22.

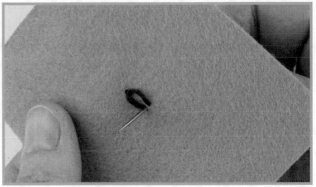

2 Bring the needle up through the work at the base of the first chain.

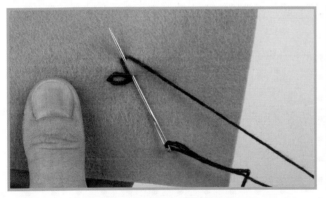

3 Make another chain stitch to the right of the first stitch.

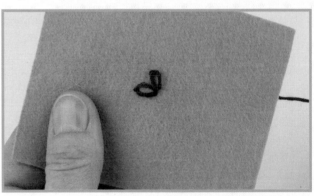

4 You now have two chains next to each other and the beginning of the lazy daisy stitch.

5 Continue making chains to the right of each stitch until you have five chains in a circle and the lazy daisy stitch is completed.

Lazy daisy stitch is used to decorate the slippers (see page 121).

KNIT ME!

It's time to make your animal! They are all the same size and they all use aran (10-ply/worsted) weight yarn, so they don't take long to make. Whichever one you choose – the bunny, mouse, monkey, kitten, puppy, panda or teddy bear – they are all equally adorable so, if you can't choose one, you might just have to make them all!

Find out how to make us in this section!

Check the measurements on pages 26 and 27 before sewing me up to ensure the clothes will fit me comfortably.

And there's a mini-me toy for each animal too!

TENSION (GAUGE)

It is worth spending some time making a tension swatch. Your tension (gauge) should be: 20 sts measured over 10cm (4in) worked in SS (stocking stitch/US stockinette stitch) and using 3.75 mm (UK 9, US 5) knitting needles.

If you are getting fewer than 20 sts, use a slightly smaller needle; if you are getting more than 20 sts, use a slightly larger needle.

Height: 20.5cm (8in)

This is my front...

Arm circumference: 9.5cm (3¾in)

Tummy circumference: 19cm (7½in)

Position the legs a stitch or two apart.

Leg length: 8cm (3³/₈in)

When you are sewing your animal together, check the measurements against those shown on these two pages to make sure the clothes will fit.

...and this is my back!

When you are putting your animal together, place the tail 2.5cm (1in) up from the bottom seam.

Mid-leg circumference: 8cm (3$\frac{1}{8}$in)

Mini-me dimensions

Height: 8.5cm (3$\frac{3}{8}$in)

BUNNY

MATERIALS

- 60m (66yd) of fluffy aran (10-ply/worsted) yarn in grey
- Small amount of pink 4-ply (fingering) yarn
- Small amount of fluffy aran (10-ply/worsted)) yarn in white
- Toy stuffing
- Two 6mm beads
- Black sewing thread

TOOLS

- Two 3.75mm (UK 9, US 5) knitting needles and a spare needle for three-needle cast-off
- 2.75mm (UK 12, US 2) knitting needles
- Sewing needle

Note:

For the bunny, the purl side of the work (WS) will be the right side.

Instructions

Body

Using grey yarn and 3.75mm (UK 9, US 5) knitting needles, cast on 18 sts and purl 1 row.
Next row: K5, M1, K8, M1, K5 (20 sts).
Next row: P5, M1, P10, M1, P5 (22 sts).
Next row: K6, M1, K10, M1, K6 (24 sts).
Next row: P6, M1, P12, M1, P6 (26 sts).
Next row: K7, M1, K12, M1, K7 (28 sts).
Next row: P7, M1, P14, M1, P7 (30 sts).
Next row: K8, M1, K14, M1, K8 (32 sts).
Next row: P8, M1, P16, M1, P8 (34 sts).
Starting with a knit row, work 12 rows in SS.
Next row: K8, ssK, K14, K2tog, K8 (32 sts).
Purl 1 row.
Next row: K7, ssK, K14, K2tog, K7 (30 sts).
Purl 1 row.
Next row: K5, (ssK) twice, K12, (K2tog), twice, K5 (26 sts).
Next row: P4, (P2tog) twice, P10, (P2togtbl) twice, P4 (22 sts).
Next row: K3, (ssK) twice, K8, (K2tog) twice, K3 (18 sts).
Purl 1 row.
Cast off.

Head

Using grey yarn and 3.75mm (UK 9, US 5) knitting needles, cast on 14 sts and, starting with a knit row, work 2 rows in SS.
Next row: (K2, M1) six times, K2 (20 sts).
Purl 1 row.
Next row: (K3, M1) six times, K2 (26 sts).
Starting with a purl row, work 5 rows in SS.
Next row: K2, (K2tog, K3) four times, K2tog, K2 (21 sts).
Starting with a purl row, work 3 rows in SS.
Next row: (K2, K2tog) five times, K1 (16 sts).
Starting with a purl row, work 3 rows in SS.

Next row: (K1, K2tog) five times, K1 (11 sts).
Purl 1 row.
Next row: (K2tog) five times, K1 (6 sts).
Thread yarn through remaining sts and leave a length for sewing up.

Leg (make two)

Using grey yarn and 3.75mm (UK 9, US 5) knitting needles, cast on 10 sts and, starting with a knit row, work 12 rows in SS.
Next row: K4, M1, K2, M1, K4 (12 sts).
Next row: P5, M1, P2, M1, P5 (14 sts).
Next row: K6, M1, K2, M1, K6 (16 sts).
Next row: P7, M1, P2, M1, P7 (18 sts).
Next row: K8, M1, K2, M1, K8 (20 sts).
Starting with a purl row, work 2 rows in SS.
Next row: P8, (P2tog) twice, P8 (18 sts).
Cast off using the three-needle cast-off technique (see page 18).

Arm (make two)

Using grey yarn and 3.75mm (UK 9, US 5) knitting needles, cast on 9 sts and, starting with a knit row, work 10 rows in SS.
Next row: (K1, M1), eight times, K1 (17 sts).
Starting with a purl row, work 7 rows in SS.
Next row: (K1, K2tog) five times, K2 (12 sts).
Next row: (P2tog) six times (6 sts).
Thread yarn through rem sts and fasten, leaving a length of yarn for sewing up.

Ear (make two)

Worked in GS.
Using grey yarn and 3.75mm (UK 9, US 5) knitting needles, cast on 2 sts and knit 1 row.
Next row: K1, M1, K1 (3 sts).
Next row: (K1, M1) twice, K1 (5 sts).
Next row: K1, M1, K1, Kfb, K1, M1, K1 (8 sts).
Knit 3 rows.
Next row: K1, M1, K6, M1, K1 (10 sts).
Knit 22 rows.
Cast off using the three-needle cast-off technique (see page 18).

Tail

Using white yarn and 3.75mm (UK 9, US 5) knitting needles, cast on 5 sts and knit 1 row.
Next row: Kfb, P3, Kfb (7 sts).
Next row: Kfb, K5, Kfb (9 sts).
Next row: Kfb, P7, Kfb (11 sts).
Starting with a knit row, work 4 rows in SS.
Next row: K2tog, K7, K2tog (9 sts).
Next row: P2tog, P5, P2tog (7 sts).
Next row: K2tog, K3, K2tog (5 sts).
Purl 1 row.
Thread yarn through sts leaving a length of yarn for sewing up.

Nose

Using pink yarn and 2.75mm (UK 12, US 2) knitting needles, cast on 5 sts and purl 1 row.
Next row: K1, M1, K3, M1, K1 (7 sts).

Purl 1 row.
Next row: ssK, K3, K2tog (5 sts).
Next row: P2tog, P1, P2togtbl (3 sts).
Next row: Sl1, K2tog, psso (1 st).
Thread yarn through remaining stitch and fasten.

Making up

Please check the diagram on page 26 for measurements before sewing your animal together to ensure the clothes will fit comfortably.

Starting with the body and remembering the WS (purl side) will be on the outside, sew the long body seam, which will be at the centre of the back. Now, with this seam in the middle, sew the cast-off edges together from side to side to form the base of the animal. Fill with toy stuffing, checking your measurements on page 26 as you go.

Taking the head, thread the yarn though the cast-off stitches, gather and secure. Sew the seam, which will be underneath the head. Fill with toy stuffing. Gather the stitches along the cast-on edge of the head and secure.

Pin the eyes in place using the photograph for guidance. Sew in place with a sewing needle and black cotton. Run the thread from the back of the eye down to the base of the head, pull slightly, and secure. Repeat for the second eye. This pulls the eyes in and gives them a much more realistic look.

Pin the nose in place and when you are happy with its placement, sew firmly in place. Using black sewing thread, embroider the mouth using straight stitches.

Pin the cast-off edge of the ears in place on the top of the head. When you are happy with their placement, sew in place.

Pin the head to the body and sew firmly in place.

Taking one of the legs, fold in half with the WS on the outside. Sew the leg seam, filling gently with toy stuffing as you go and checking the measurements on page 26. The long seam will be at the back of the leg. Sew the seam at the top of the leg together, placing the back leg seam in the middle of this seam. Repeat for second leg.

Taking one of the arms, gather the cast-off edge and sew the seam, filling gently with toy stuffing as you go and checking your measurements. The seam will be underneath the arm. Sew the cast-on edge together. Repeat for the second arm.

Pin the arms in place onto the sides of the body using the photograph for guidance. Sew in place.

Pin the legs in place onto the body using the photographs for guidance and sew in place.

Taking the tail, run the yarn through the stitches around the outside edge of the tail. Gather and place a small amount of toy stuffing inside. Tighten the yarn and secure.

Sew the tail in place on the back of the body using the photograph for guidance and the instructions on page 27.

BUNNY MINI-ME

Instructions

Legs and body

Using grey yarn, cast on 5 sts and work as follows.
Next row: K2, M1, K1, M1, K2 (7 sts).
Next row: P1, P2tog, P1, P2togtbl, P1 (5 sts).
Starting with a knit row, work 4 rows in SS.
Cast off 1 st at the beginning of the next two rows (3 sts).*
Break yarn and leave sts on a spare needle or stitch holder.
Make a second leg by working from the beginning of the instructions to *.
With RS facing, place both legs on your needle and cast on 3 sts at the beginning of the row.
Knit these 3 sts, K2 from the first leg stitches, M1, K2tog (last st from the first leg and the first stitch from the second leg), M1, K2 (10 sts).
Next row: Cast on 3 sts, P5, M1, P3, M1, P5 (15 sts).
Starting with a knit row, work 4 rows in SS.
Next row: K2, ssK, K7, K2tog, K2 (13 sts).
Purl 1 row.
Next row: K2, ssK, K5, K2tog, K2 (11 sts).
Purl 1 row.
Next row: K1, (K2tog) five times (6 sts).
Thread yarn through sts, leaving a length for sewing up.

MATERIALS

- Small amount of fluffy aran (10-ply/worsted) yarn in grey
- Small amount of fluffy aran (10-ply/worsted) yarn in white
- Small amount of 4-ply (fingering) yarn in pink
- Two 4mm beads
- Toy stuffing
- Black sewing thread

TOOLS

- 3.75mm (UK 9, US 5) knitting needles
- Sewing needle
- Stitch holder or spare knitting needle

Head

The cast-on edge forms the nose.
Using grey yarn, cast on 4 sts.
Next row: (K1, M1) three times, K1 (7 sts).
Purl 1 row.
Next row: K1, M1, K2, M1, K1, M1, K2, M1, K1 (11 sts).
Next row: Purl 1 row.
Next row: K5, M1, K1, M1, K5 (13 sts).
Purl 1 row.
Next row: (K1, K2tog) four times, K1 (9 sts).
Purl 1 row.
Next row: (K2tog) four times, K1 (5 sts).
Thread yarn through remaining sts and fasten, leaving a length of yarn for sewing up.

Arm (make two)

Using grey yarn, cast on 4 sts and work 6 rows in SS.
Thread yarn through sts and fasten, leaving a length of yarn for sewing up. You cannot use the i-cord technique for the arms as the WS will be on the outside.

Ear (make two)

Using grey yarn, cast on 1 st.
Next row: Kfb (2 sts).
Next row: K1, M1, K1 (3 sts).
Next row: (K1, M1) twice, K1 (5 sts).
Next row: K1, M1, K3, M1, K1 (7 sts).
Knit 8 rows.
Next row: K3, K2tog, K2 (6 sts).
Cast off using the three-needle cast-off technique, leaving a length of yarn for sewing the ear in place.

Tail

Using white yarn, cast on 1 st.
Next row: Kfbf (3 sts).
Starting with a knit row, work 3 rows in SS.
Thread yarn through sts, thread yarn around the edge of the work and gather to make a bobble with the purl side (WS) on the outside.

Making up

Starting with one of the legs, thread yarn through the cast-on sts and gather to close. Sew the back leg seam, filling with toy stuffing as you go. Repeat for the second leg.

Working from the cast-off edge (neck edge) of the body, gather the cast-off sts and sew the seam which will be at the back of the body. Fill with toy stuffing.

Make a few stitches through the body at the top of each leg to add definition, using the photographs for guidance.

Taking the head, and with the WS on the outside, gather the cast-off stitches and fasten. Sew the seam, which will be underneath the head. Fill with toy stuffing. Thread the yarn through the cast-on stitches, gather and secure.

Pin the ears in place. When you are happy with their placement, sew them securely in place. Taking a sewing needle and black cotton, sew each eye in place, using the photograph as guidance. Using pink 4-ply (fingering) yarn, embroider the nose using straight stitches. Sew the head to the body securely.

Taking the arms, pin in place and sew to the body, taking the needle from one side, through the body and second arm and back again. This will ensure the arms 'pivot' and can move up and down. Secure yarn.

Sew the tail to the back of the body.

The mini-me animals are all the same size and their making up instructions are very similar.

MOUSE

Instructions

Body

Using grey tweed yarn, follow the instructions for the Bunny on page 28

Head

Using grey tweed yarn and 3.75mm (UK 9, US 5) knitting needles, cast on 6 sts and purl 1 row.
Next row: (K1, M1) twice, K2, (M1, K1) twice (10 sts).
Purl 1 row.
Next row: K1, M1, K3, M1, K2, M1, K3, M1, K1 (14 sts).
Purl 1 row.
Next row: K6, M1, K2, M1, K6 (16 sts).
Purl 1 row.
Next row: K1, M1, K6, M1, K2, M1, K6, M1, K1 (20 sts).
Purl 1 row.
Next row: K9, M1, K2, M1, K9 (22 sts).
Purl 1 row.
Next row: K1, M1, K9, M1, K2, M1, K9, M1, K1 (26 sts).
Purl 1 row.
Next row: K12, M1, K2, M1, K12 (28 sts).
Starting with a purl row, work 5 rows in SS.
Next row: (K2, K2tog) seven times (21 sts).
Purl 1 row.
Next row: (K1, K2tog) seven times (14 sts).
Purl 1 row.
Thread yarn through remaining sts, leaving a length of yarn for sewing up.

Arm (make two)

Using grey tweed yarn, follow the instructions on page 28.

Leg (make two)

Using grey tweed yarn, follow the instructions on page 28.

Ear (make two)

Using grey tweed yarn and 3.75mm (UK 9, US 5) knitting needles, cast on 3 sts and purl 1 row.
Next row: (K1, M1) twice, K1 (5 sts).
Purl 1 row.
Next row: K1, M1, K to last st, M1, K1 (7 sts).
Starting with a purl row, work 3 rows in SS.
Next row: ssK, K3, K2tog (5 sts).

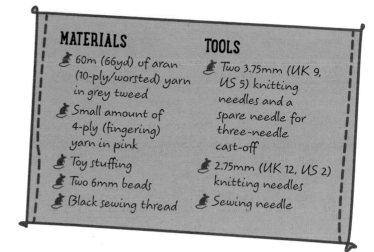

MATERIALS

- 60m (66yd) of aran (10-ply/worsted) yarn in grey tweed
- Small amount of 4-ply (fingering) yarn in pink
- Toy stuffing
- Two 6mm beads
- Black sewing thread

TOOLS

- Two 3.75mm (UK 9, US 5) knitting needles and a spare needle for three-needle cast-off
- 2.75mm (UK 12, US 2) knitting needles
- Sewing needle

Purl 1 row.
Next row: ssK, K1, K2tog (3 sts).
Next row: Sl1, P2tog, psso (1 st).
Thread yarn through rem sts and fasten, leaving a length of yarn for sewing up.

Ear lining (make two)

Using pink yarn and 2.75mm (UK 12, US 2) knitting needles, cast on 5 sts and purl 1 row.
Next row: K1, M1, K to last st, M1, K1 (7 sts).
Purl 1 row.
Repeat last two rows twice more (11 sts).
Starting with a knit row, work 4 rows in SS.
Next row: ssK, K7, K2tog (9 sts).
Purl 1 row.
Next row: ssK, K5, K2tog (7 sts).
Next row: P2tog, P3, P2togtbl (5 sts).
Next row: ssK, K1, K2tog (3 sts).
Cast off purlwise, leaving a length of yarn for sewing up.

Ear edging (make two)

If you do not want to use the i-cord technique the edgings can be knitted flat and the side seam sewn together before sewing to the ear edge.
Using grey tweed yarn and 3.75mm (UK 9, US 5) DPN, cast on 3 sts and work an i-cord as follows:
1 Knit all the stitches.
2 Slide the stitches to the other end of the needle.
3 Pulling the yarn around the back of the stitches, knit the stitches again
Repeat steps 2 and 3. By pulling the yarn behind the stitches on the needle, you close the 'gap' and give the fabric the appearance of French knitting.
Work until the i-cord, when slightly stretched, fits around the outside edge of the ear (approximately 10cm/4in). Do not cast off and leave a length of yarn in case you need to adjust the length once sewn around the edge of the ear.

Tail

Using grey tweed yarn and 3.75mm (UK 9, US 5) knitting needles, cast on 4 sts and work an i-cord in SS until tail measures 12cm (4¾in).

Thread yarn through sts, leaving a length of yarn for sewing up.

Nose

Using pink yarn and 2.75mm (UK 12, US 2) knitting needles, cast on 5 sts and, starting with a knit row, work 2 rows in SS.

Next row: K1, M1, K3, M1, K1 (7 sts).

Starting with a purl row work 3 rows in SS.

Next row: ssK, K3, K2tog (5 sts).

Purl 1 row.

Cast off.

Making up

Please check the diagram on page 26 for measurements before sewing your animal together to ensure the clothes will fit comfortably.

Sew up and stuff the body and head, and sew the eyes in place following the instructions on page 30. Taking the nose, thread the yarn through the stitches around the outside edge, gather, placing a small amount of toy stuffing inside and secure. Sew in place using the photograph for guidance.

Taking one ear and one i-cord ear edging, sew the ear edging in place using the photograph as guidance and sewing to the stitches around the outside edge of the ear. The cast-on edge forms the bottom of the ear. The WS will form the inside of the ear. Adjust the length of the i-cord if necessary. Thread the yarn through the stitches, gather and fasten off. Using pink yarn and with the RS facing outwards, sew the ear lining to the inside (WS) of the ear, just underneath the i-cord edging. Repeat for the second ear.

Pin the cast-on edge of the ears in place on the top of the head and sew in place.

Sew up and stuff the arms and legs, and then sew them to the body following the instructions on page 30.

Taking the tail, sew the ends of yarn in and sew to the back of the body, placing it approximately 2.5cm (1in) from the bottom seam.

MOUSE MINI-ME

Instructions

Legs and body

Using grey yarn, follow the instructions for the Bunny Mini-me on page 31.

Head

Using grey yarn, follow the instructions on page 31 for the Bunny Mini-me.

Arm (make two)

Using grey yarn, follow the instructions on page 31 for the Bunny Mini-me.

Ear (make two)

Knitted in GS.
Using grey yarn, cast on 3 sts and knit 1 row.
Next row: Kfb, K1, Kfb (5 sts).
Knit 1 row.
Next row: Kfb, K3, Kfb (7 sts).
Knit 1 row.
Next row: (K1, K2tog) twice, K1 (5 sts).
Next row: K2tog, K1, K2tog (3 sts).
Cast off.

Tail

Using grey yarn, cast on 2 sts and, using the i-cord technique (see page 33 under *Ear edging*), work in SS until tail measures 4cm (1½in).
Thread yarn through sts, leaving a length of yarn for sewing the tail to the body.

MATERIALS
- Small amount of tweed aran (10-ply/worsted) yarn in grey
- Small amount of 4-ply (fingering) yarn in pink
- Two 4mm beads
- Toy stuffing
- Black sewing thread

TOOLS
- 3.75mm (UK 9, US 5) DPN
- Sewing needle
- Stitch holder or spare knitting needle

Making up

Sew up and stuff the legs and body following the instructions on page 32. Sew up and stuff the head following the instructions on page 32. Pin the ears in position and sew them securely in place. Taking a sewing needle and black cotton, sew each bead in place for the eyes, using the photograph for guidance. Using pink yarn, embroider the nose using straight stitches.

Sew the head to the body securely. Follow the instructions on page 32 to sew the arms in place. Sew the tail to the back of the body.

MONKEY

MATERIALS

- 55m (60yd) aran (10-ply/worsted) yarn in dark brown
- 15m (16yd) aran (10-ply/worsted) yarn in rust brown
- Small amount of 4-ply (fingering) yarn in black
- Toy stuffing
- Two 6mm black beads
- Black sewing thread

TOOLS

- Two 3.75mm (UK 9, US 5) knitting needles and a spare needle for three-needle cast-off
- 2.75mm (UK 12, US 2) knitting needles
- Sewing needle

Note:

The parts knitted using dark brown will be sewn together with the purl side (WS) on the outside, meaning that the parts knitted using rust brown will have the knit side (RS) on the outside.

Instructions

Body

Using dark brown yarn, follow the instructions for the Bunny on page 28.

Head

Using dark brown yarn and 3.75mm (UK 9, US 5) knitting needles, cast on 12 sts and purl 1 row.
Next row: (K3, M1) three times, K3 (15 sts).
Purl 1 row.
Next row: K5, M1, K5, M1, K5 (17 sts).
Purl 1 row.
Next row: K5, M1, K7, M1, K5 (19 sts).
Next row: P5, M1, P9, M1, P5 (21 sts).
Starting with a knit row, work 4 rows in SS.
Next row: K6, M1, K9, M1, K6 (23 sts).
Starting with a purl row, work 5 rows in SS.
Next row: (K3, K2tog) four times, K3 (19 sts).
Purl 1 row.
Next row: (K2, K2tog) four times, K3 (15 sts).

Next row: (P2tog) seven times, P1 (8 sts).
Thread yarn through remaining sts and leave a length for sewing up.

Face section

Using rust brown yarn and 3.75mm (UK 9, US 5) knitting needles, cast on 10 sts and, starting with a knit row, work 4 rows in SS.
Next row: ssK, K to last 2 sts, K2tog (8 sts).
Purl 1 row.
Repeat last two rows once more (6 sts).
Next row: K1, M1, K to last st, M1, K1 (8 sts).
Purl 1 row.
Repeat last two rows once more (10 sts).
Starting with a knit row, work 4 rows in SS.
Cast off.
Sew the small side seams together with the RS on the outside and, using rust brown yarn and 3.75mm (UK 9, US 5) knitting needles, pick up and knit 6 sts along the centre of the top edge of the face section.
Next row: P1, M1, P4, M1, P1 (8 sts).
Starting with a knit row, work 2 rows in SS.
Next row: K4, turn and working only over these 4 sts, work as follows:
*Purl 1 row.
Next row: ssK, K2tog (making 2 sts), pick up the first stitch and lift it over the second stitch to cast off on this row. Thread yarn through the remaining stitch and fasten*.
With RS facing, rejoin yarn to remaining 4 sts, knit 1 row and then work from * to * once more.

Leg (make two)

Using dark brown yarn and 3.75mm (UK 9, US 5) knitting needles, cast on 10 sts and, starting with a purl row, work 12 rows in SS.
Change to rust brown yarn.
Next row: K4, M1, K2, M1, K4 (12 sts).
Next row: P5, M1, P2, M1, P5 (14 sts).
Next row: K6, M1, K2, M1, K6 (16 sts).
Next row: P7, M1, P2, M1, P7 (18 sts).
Next row: K8, M1, K2, M1, K8 (20 sts).
Starting with a purl row, work 3 rows in SS.
Next row: K8, ssK, K2tog, K8 (18 sts).
Cast off using the three-needle cast-off technique (see page 18), making sure that the knit side of the foot will be on the outside.

Arm (make two)

Using dark brown yarn and 3.75mm (UK 9, US 5) knitting needles, cast on 9 sts and, starting with a knit row, work 10 rows in SS.
Next row: (K1, M1), eight times, K1 (17 sts).
Change to rust brown yarn and, starting with a knit row, work 6 rows in SS.

Next row: (K1, K2tog) five times, K2 (12 sts).
Next row. (P2tog) six times (6 sts).
Thread yarn through rem sts and fasten.

Ear (make two)

Using dark brown yarn and 3.75mm (UK 9, US 5) needles cast on 5 sts and, starting with a knit row, work 2 rows in SS.
Next row: K4, w&t (see page 14).
Next row: P3, w&t.
Next row: K3, w&t.
Next row: Purl to end of row.
Starting with a knit row, work 2 rows in SS.
Cast off.

Nose

Using black yarn and 2.75mm (UK 12, US 2) knitting needles, cast on 4 sts and purl 1 row.
Next row: K1, M1, K2, M1, K1 (6 sts).

Purl 1 row.
Next row: ssK, K2, K2tog (4 sts).
Purl 1 row.
Cast off.

Tail

Using dark brown aran yarn and 3.75mm (UK 9, US 5) needles, cast on 5 sts and, starting with a knit row, work 4 rows in SS.
*Next row: K4, w&t.
Next row: P3, w&t.
Next row. knit to end of row.
Starting with a purl row work 5 rows in SS*.
Repeat from * to * twice more.
*Next row: K4, w&t.
Next row: P3, w&t.
Next row: knit to end of row.
Starting with a purl row work 3 rows in SS*.
Repeat from * to * twice more.
Thread yarn through remaining sts, leaving a length of yarn for sewing up.

Making up

Please check the diagram on page 26 for measurements before sewing your animal together to ensure the clothes will fit comfortably.

Sew up and stuff the body following the instructions on page 30.

All pieces knitted using dark brown yarn will have the WS facing outwards.

Taking the head, thread your yarn though the cast-off stitches, gather and secure. The cast-off edge forms the bottom of the head. Sew the seam, which will be at the back of the head. Fill with toy stuffing. Gather the stitches along the cast-on edge of the head and secure.

Taking the face section in rust brown, place some toy stuffing inside and pin in place, using the photographs for guidance. Sew in place, sewing around each eye section.

Sew the eyes and nose in place following the instructions on page 30. Using black yarn, embroider the mouth with straight stitches.

Fold one of the ears in half with the purl side (WS) on the outside. Sew around the outside edge of the ear. Repeat for second ear. Pin the ears in place on the head so that the fold is on the ear. When you are happy with their position, sew in place.

Pin the head to the body and sew firmly in place.

Matching the yarn colours, sew the legs and arms together following the instructions on page 30.

Sew up and stuff the arms and legs and attach to the body following the instructions on page 30.

Sew the seam of the tail and pin it in place on the back of the body approximately 2.5cm (1in) from the bottom seam, then sew it in position.

MONKEY MINI-ME

MATERIALS

- Small amount of aran (10-ply/worsted) yarn in dark brown
- Small amount of aran (10-ply/worsted) yarn in rust brown
- Small amount of 4-ply (fingering) yarn in black
- Two 4mm beads
- Toy stuffing
- Black sewing thread

TOOLS

- 3.75mm (UK 9, US 5) DPN
- Sewing needle
- Stitch holder or spare knitting needle

Instructions

Legs and body

Using dark brown yarn, follow instructions for the Bunny Mini-me on page 31.

Head

Using dark brown yarn, cast on 7 sts.
Next row: (K1, M1) six times, K1 (13 sts).
Starting with a purl row, work 9 rows in SS.
Next row: (K2tog) six times, K1 (7 sts).
Thread yarn through remaining sts and fasten, leaving a length of yarn for sewing up.

Face section

Using rust brown yarn, cast on 5 sts and, starting with a knit row, work 2 rows in SS.
Next row: K4, w&t (see page 14).
Next row: P3, w&t.
Next row: K3, w&t.
Next row: P3, w&t.
Next row: Knit to end of row.
Purl 1 row.
Next row: Cast off.
With RS facing and rust brown yarn, pick up 4 sts along the cast off-edge.
Starting with a purl row, work 2 rows in SS.
Next row: P2tog, P2togtbl (2 sts).
Lift first stitch over second stitch to cast off. Thread yarn through remaining st and fasten.

Arm (make two)

Using dark brown yarn, follow instructions on page 31 for the Bunny Mini-me.

Ear (make two)

Using dark brown yarn, cast on 4 sts and knit 2 rows.
Next row: (K2tog) twice (2 sts).
Lift first stitch over second stitch to cast off. Thread yarn through remaining st and fasten.

Tail

Using dark brown yarn, cast on 14 sts.
Next row: Cast off.

Making up

Note: All dark brown pieces are sewn together with the WS on the outside.

Sew up and stuff the legs and body following the instructions on page 32.

With the WS on the outside, gather the cast-off stitches of the head and fasten. Sew the seam, which will be at the back of the head. Fill with toy stuffing. Thread the yarn through the cast-on stitches, gather and secure. The cast-off edge forms the bottom of the head.

Taking the face section, sew the small side seams. Place a small amount of toy stuffing inside and pin in place, using the photographs for guidance. Sew the face section in place, ensuring the eye piece is flat. Taking a sewing needle and black cotton, sew each eye in place, using the photographs as guidance.

Taking an ear, pin in place with the cast-on edge on the side of the head. Repeat for the second ear. When you are happy with their position, sew securely in place.

Using black yarn, embroider the nose and mouth using straight stitches. Securely sew the head to the body.

Follow the instructions on page 32 to sew the arms in place. Sew the tail to the back of the body.

KITTEN

MATERIALS

- 60m (66yd) of aran (10-ply/worsted) yarn in ginger
- Small amount of 4-ply (fingering) yarn in pink
- Toy stuffing
- Two black 6mm beads
- Black sewing thread

TOOLS

- Two 3.75mm (UK 9, US 5) knitting needles and a spare needle for three-needle cast-off
- 2.75mm (UK 12, US 2) knitting needles
- Sewing needle

Note:

The purl side of the work (WS) will be the right side.

Instructions

Body

Using ginger yarn, follow the instructions for the Bunny on page 28.

Head

The cast-on edge forms the nose.

Using ginger yarn and 3.75mm (UK 9, US 5) knitting needles, cast on 12 sts and purl 1 row.

Next row: (K3, M1) three times, K3 (15 sts).

Purl 1 row.

Next row: K4, M1, K3, M1, K1, M1, K3, M1, K4 (19 sts).

Purl 1 row.

Next row: K5, M1, K4, M1, K1, M1, K4, M1, K5 (23 sts).

Purl 1 row.

Next row: K6, M1, K5, M1, K1, M1, K5, M1, K6 (27 sts).

Purl 1 row.

Next row: K11, ssK, K1, K2tog, K11 (25 sts).

Next row: P10, P2tog, P1, P2togtbl, P10 (23 sts).

Next row: K9, ssK, K1, K2tog, K9 (21 sts).

Purl 1 row.

Next row: K4, ssK, K9, K2tog, K4 (19 sts).

Purl 1 row.

Next row: K4, ssK, K7, K2tog, K4 (17 sts).

Next row: P3, P2tog, P7, P2togtbl, P3 (15 sts).

Next row: K3, ssK, K5, K2tog, K3 (13 sts).

Next row: P2, P2tog, P5, P2togtbl, P2 (11 sts).

Thread yarn through remaining sts, leaving a length for sewing up.

Ear (make four)

Using ginger yarn and 3.75mm (UK 9, US 5) knitting needles, cast on 5 sts and, starting with a knit row, work 2 rows in SS.

Next row: ssK, K1, K2tog (3 sts).

Purl 1 row.

Next row: sl 2sts as if to knit together, K1, psso (1 st).

Thread yarn through remaining st and fasten.

Arm (make two)

Using ginger yarn, follow the instructions on page 28 for the Bunny.

Leg (make two)

Using ginger yarn, follow the instructions on page 28 for the Bunny.

Tail

Using ginger yarn and 3.75mm (UK 9, US 5) knitting needles, cast on 7 sts and, starting with a knit row, work 8 rows in SS.

*Next row: K5, w&t (see page 14).

Next row: P3, w&t.

Next row: Knit to end of row.

Starting with a purl row, work 5 rows in SS*.

Work from * to * once more.

Next row: K1, ssK, K1, K2tog, K1 (5 sts).

Purl 1 row.

Thread yarn through sts and fasten.

Nose

Using pink yarn and 2.75mm (UK 12, US 2) knitting needles, cast on 6 sts and, starting with a knit row, work 2 rows in SS.

Next row: ssK, K2, K2tog (4 sts).

Purl 1 row.

Next row: ssK, K2tog (2 sts).

Next row: P2tog (1 st).

Thread yarn through remaining st and fasten.

Making up

Note: All pieces are sewn together with the purl side (WS) on the outside.

Please check the diagram on page 26 for measurements before sewing your animal together to ensure the clothes will fit comfortably.

Sew up and stuff the body and head, and sew the eyes and nose in place following the instructions on page 30.

Place two ear pieces with RS together, and sew them together. If you trim the ends of yarn, you can 'hide' them inside the ear as you sew the pieces together. Repeat for the second ear. Pin the ears in place so that the cast-off edge is at the top of each ear and sew in place. Pin the head to the body and sew firmly in place.

Sew up and stuff the arms and legs, and then sew them to the body following the instructions on page 30.

Gather the cast-off stitches of the tail and then sew along the long seam, filling with toy stuffing as you go. Sew the tail in place on the back of the body approximately 2.5cm (1in) from the bottom seam.

KITTEN MINI-ME

Instructions

Legs and body

Using ginger yarn, follow the instructions on page 31 for the Bunny Mini-me.

Head

Using ginger yarn, follow the instructions on page 31 for the Bunny Mini-me.

Arm (make two)

Using ginger yarn, follow the instructions on page 31 for the Bunny Mini-me.

Ear (make two)

Using ginger yarn, cast on 4 sts and purl 1 row.
Next row: (K2tog) twice (2 sts).
Next row: P2tog (1 st).
Thread yarn through remaining st to secure, leaving a length of yarn for sewing the ear to the head.

Tail

Using ginger yarn, cast on 2 sts and, using the i-cord technique (see page 33 under *Ear edging*), work in SS until the tail measures 4cm (1½in).
Thread yarn through stitches to secure, leaving a length of yarn for sewing the tail to the body.

MATERIALS

- Small amount of aran (10-ply/worsted) yarn in ginger
- Small amount of 4-ply (fingering) yarn in pink
- Toy stuffing
- Two 4mm beads
- Black sewing thread

TOOLS

- 3.75mm (UK 9, US 5) DPN
- Sewing needle
- Stitch holder or spare knitting needle

Making up

Note: All pieces are sewn together with the purl side (WS) on the outside.

Sew up and stuff the legs and body following the instructions on page 32.

Sew up and stuff the head following the instructions on page 32. Pin the ears in position and sew them securely in place. Taking a sewing needle and black cotton, sew each bead in place for the eyes, using the photograph for guidance.

With pink yarn, embroider the nose using straight stitches and, using black yarn, embroider the whiskers. Sew the head securely to the body. Follow the instructions on page 32 to sew the arms in place. Sew the tail to the back of the body.

PUPPY

Instructions

Body

Using brown yarn, follow the instructions on page 28 for the Bunny.

Tummy

Using cream yarn and 3.75mm (UK 9, US 5) knitting needles, cast on 5 sts and purl 1 row.
Next row: K1, M1, K3, M1, K1 (7 sts).
Next row: P1, M1, P5, M1, P1 (9 sts).
Next row: K1, M1, K7, M1, K1 (11 sts).
Starting with a purl row work 3 rows in SS.
Next row: K1, ssK, K to last 3 sts, K2tog, K1 (9 sts).
Purl 1 row.
Repeat last two rows once more (7 sts).
Starting with a knit row, work 2 rows in SS.
Next row: K1, ssK, K1, K2tog, K1 (5 sts).
Starting with a purl row, work 3 rows in SS.
Next row: ssK, K1, K2tog (3 sts).
Next row (WS): Cast off.

Head

Using cream yarn and 3.75mm (UK 9, US 5) knitting needles, cast on 5 sts.
Next row: (K1, M1) four times, K1 (9 sts).
Purl 1 row.
Next row: (K1, M1) eight times, K1 (17 sts).
Starting with a purl row, work 3 rows in SS.
Change to brown yarn and cont in SS.
Next row: K5, ssK, K3, K2tog, K5 (15 sts).
Purl 1 row.
Next row: K1, M1, K5, M1, K3, M1, K5, M1, K1 (19 sts).
Next row: P8, M1, P3, M1, P8 (21 sts).
Next row: K9, M1, K3, M1, K9 (23 sts).
Next row: P10, M1, P3, M1, P10 (25 sts).
Next row: K11, M1, K3, M1, K11 (27 sts).
Next row: P12, M1, P3, M1, P12 (29 sts).
Next row: K13, M1, K3, M1, K13 (31 sts).
Starting with a purl row, work 5 rows in SS.
Next row: K12, ssK, K3, K2tog, SK, K12 (29 sts).
Next row: P1, P2tog, P23, P2togtbl, P1 (27 sts).
Next row: K1, ssK, K7, K2tog, K3, ssK, K7, K2tog, K1 (23 sts).
Purl 1 row.

MATERIALS

 55m (60yd) tweed aran (10-ply/worsted) yarn in brown

 15m (16.5yd) tweed aran (10-ply/worsted) yarn in cream

 Small amount of 4-ply (fingering) yarn in black

 Toy stuffing

 Two 6mm beads

 Black sewing thread

TOOLS

 Two 3.75mm (UK 9, US 5) knitting needles and a spare needle for three-needle cast-off

 2.75mm (UK 12, US 2) knitting needles

 Sewing needle

Next row: K1, ssK, K5, K2tog, K3, ssK, K5, K2tog, K1 (19 sts).
Next row: P1, P2tog, P3, P2togtbl, P3, P2tog, P3, P2togtbl, P1 (15 sts).
Next row: K7, K2tog, K6 (14 sts).
Divide the remaining stitches over two needles and cast off using the three-needle cast-off technique (see page 18).

Leg (make two)

Using brown yarn, follow instructions on page 28 for the Bunny, changing to cream yarn after the first 12 SS rows.

Arm (make two)

Using brown yarn, follow instructions on page 28 for the Bunny, changing to cream yarn after the first 10 rows in SS.

Ear (make two)

Using brown yarn and 3.75mm (UK 9, US 5) knitting needles, cast on 5 sts and, starting with a knit row, work 2 rows in SS.
Next row: K1, M1, K3, M1, K1 (7 sts).
Starting with a purl row work 11 rows in SS.
Next row: ssK, K3, K2tog (5 sts).
Next row: P2tog, P1, P2togtbl (3 sts).
Cast off.

Ear lining (make two)

Using cream yarn and 3.75mm (UK 9, US 5) knitting needles, cast on 4 sts and purl 1 row.
Next row: K1, M1, K2, M1, K1 (6 sts).
Starting with a purl row, work 11 rows in SS.
Next row: ssK, K2, K2tog (4 sts).
Next row: P2tog, P2togtbl (2 sts).
Pass one stitch over the other to cast off.

Tail

Using brown yarn and 3.75mm (UK 9, US 5) knitting needles, cast on 7 sts and, starting with a knit row, work 6 rows in SS.
Next row: K1, ssK, K1, K2tog, K1 (5 sts).
Purl 1 row.
Change to cream yarn and, continuing in SS, work 2 rows.
Next row: ssK, K1, K2tog. (3 sts).
Purl 1 row.
Thread yarn through sts leaving a length of yarn for sewing up.

Nose

Using black yarn and 2.75mm (UK 12, US 2) knitting needles, cast on 4 sts and purl 1 row.
Next row: K1, M1, K2, M1, K1 (6 sts).
Purl 1 row.
Next row: ssK, K2, K2tog (4 sts).
Next row: P2tog, P2togtbl (2 sts).
Pass one stitch over the other to cast off.

Making up

Check the diagram on page 26 for measurements before sewing the animal together to ensure the clothes will fit comfortably.

Sew up and stuff the body and head following the instructions on page 30.

Pin the tummy in place, using the photographs for guidance, and sew carefully to the body.

Sew the eyes and nose in place following the instructions on page 30.

Taking an ear and ear lining, sew together with the WS together. Repeat for the second ear. Pin the cast-off edge of the ears in place on the top of the head. When you are happy with their position, sew in place.

Pin the head to the body and sew firmly in place.

Sew up and stuff the arms and legs, then sew them in place following the instructions on page 30.

Run the yarn through the stitches around the outside edge of the tail, gather and place a small amount of toy stuffing inside. Tighten the yarn and secure. Sew the tail in place on the back of the body approximately 2.5cm (1in) from the bottom seam.

PUPPY MINI-ME

Instructions

Legs and body

Using brown yarn, follow the instructions on page 31 for the Bunny Mini-me.

Head

Using cream yarn, cast on 4 sts.
Next row: (K1, M1) three times, K1 (7 sts).
Purl 1 row.
Change to brown yarn.
Next row: K1, M1, K2, M1, K1, M1, K2, M1, K1 (11 sts).
Purl 1 row.
Next row: K5, M1, K1, M1, K5 (13 sts).
Purl 1 row.
Next row: (K1, K2tog) four times, K1 (9 sts).
Purl 1 row.
Next row: (K2tog) four times, K1 (5 sts).
Thread yarn through remaining sts and fasten, leaving a length of yarn for sewing up.

Arm (make two)

Using brown yarn, follow the instructions on page 31 for the Bunny Mini-me.

Ear (make two)

Using brown yarn cast on 2 sts.
Purl 1 row.
Next row: K1, M1, K1 (3 sts).
Starting with a purl row, work 5 rows in SS.
Cast off, leaving a length of yarn for sewing up.

Tail

Using brown yarn, cast on 3 sts and, using the i-cord technique (see page 33 under *Ear edging*), work 2 rows in SS.
Next row: K1, K2tog (2 sts).
Thread yarn through remaining sts and fasten.

MATERIALS

- Small amount of tweed aran (10-ply/ worsted) yarn in brown
- Small amount of tweed aran (10-ply/worsted) yarn in cream
- Small amount of 4-ply (fingering) yarn in black
- Two 4mm beads
- Toy stuffing
- Black sewing thread

TOOLS

- 3.75mm (UK 9, US 5) DPN
- Sewing needle
- Stitch holder or spare knitting needle

Making up

Using matching yarn throughout, Sew up and stuff the legs and body following the instructions on page 32.

Sew up and stuff the head following the instructions on page 32. Pin the ears to the head and sew them securely in place. Taking a sewing needle and black cotton, sew each bead in place for eyes, using the photograph as guidance. Using black yarn, embroider the nose using straight stitches. Sew the head firmly to the body.

Follow the instructions on page 32 to sew the arms in place. Sew the tail to the back of the body.

PANDA

Instructions

Body

Using black yarn and 3.75mm (UK 9, US 5) knitting needles cast on 18 sts and purl 1 row.
Next row: K5, M1, K8, M1, K5 (20 sts).
Next row: P5, M1, P10, M1, P5 (22 sts).
Next row: K6, M1, K10, M1, K6 (24 sts).
Next row: P6, M1, P12, M1, P6 (26 sts).
Next row: K7, M1, K12, M1, K7 (28 sts).
Next row: P7, M1, P14, M1, P7 (30 sts).
Next row: K8, M1, K14, M1, K8 (32 sts).
Next row: P8, M1, P16, M1, P8 (34 sts).
Change to white yarn and starting with a knit row, work 12 rows in SS.
Next row: K8, ssK, K14, K2tog, K8 (32 sts).
Purl 1 row.
Next row: K7, ssK, K14, K2tog, K7 (30 sts).
Purl 1 row.
Next row: K5, (ssK) twice, K12, (K2tog), twice, K5 (26 sts).
Next row: P4, (P2tog) twice, P10, (P2togtbl), twice, P4 (22 sts).
Next row: K3, (ssK) twice, K8, (K2tog), twice, K3 (18 sts).
Purl 1 row.
Cast off.

Head

Using white yarn and 3.75mm (UK 9, US 5) knitting needles, cast on 8 sts and purl 1 row.
Next row: (K1, M1) seven times, K1 (15 sts).
Starting with a purl row, work 3 rows in SS.
Cast off and, with RS facing, pick up and knit 15 sts.
Purl 1 row.
Next row: K3, (Kfb) nine times, K3 (24 sts).
Purl 1 row.
Next row: (K8, M1) twice, K8 (26 sts).
Purl 1 row.
Next row: K1, M1, (K8, M1) three times, K1 (30 sts).
Purl 1 row.
Next row: K1, M1, K9, M1, K10, M1, K9, M1, K1 (34 sts).
Starting with a purl row, work 3 rows in SS.
Next row: (K3, K2tog) six times, K4 (28 sts).
Purl 1 row.

MATERIALS

- 55m (60yd) fluffy aran (10-ply/worsted) yarn in black
- 30m (33yd) fluffy aran (10-ply/worsted) yarn in white
- Small amount of 4-ply (fingering) yarn in black
- Toy stuffing
- Two 6mm beads
- Black sewing thread

TOOLS

- Two 3.75mm (UK 9, US 5) knitting needles and a spare needle for three-needle cast-off
- 2.75mm (UK 12, US 2) knitting needles
- Sewing needle

Next row: (K2, K2tog) seven times (21 sts).
Purl 1 row.
Next row: (K1, K2tog) seven times (14 sts).
Purl 1 row.
Thread yarn through remaining sts and leave a length for sewing up.

Leg (make two)

Using black yarn, follow the instructions on page 28 for the Bunny.

Arm (make two)

Using black yarn, follow the instructions on page 28 for the Bunny.

Ear (make two)

Using black yarn and 3.75mm (UK 9, US 5) knitting needles, cast on 5 sts and, starting with a knit row, work 2 rows in SS.
Next row: K4, w&t (see page 14).
Next row: P3, w&t.
Next row: K3, w&t.
Next row: P3, w&t.
Next row: Knit to the end of the row.
Starting with a purl row, work 3 rows in SS.
Cast off.

Eye piece (make two)

Using black yarn and 3.75mm (UK 9, US 5) knitting needles, cast on 2 sts and, starting with a knit row, work 2 rows in SS.
Next row: K1, M1, K1 (3 sts).
Starting with a purl row, work 2 rows in SS.
Next row: Sl1, P2tog, psso (1 st).
Thread yarn through remaining stitch and fasten.

Nose

Using black 4-ply (fingering) yarn and 2.75mm (UK 12, US 2) knitting needles, cast on 4 sts and, starting with a knit row, work 3 rows in SS.
Next row: (P2tog) twice (2 sts).
Thread yarn through remaining stitches, leaving a length of yarn for sewing up.

Tail

Using black aran (10-ply/worsted) yarn and 3.75mm (UK 9, US 5) knitting needles, cast on 4 sts and, starting with a knit row, work 2 rows in SS.
Next row: K3, w&t.
Next row: P2, w&t.
Next row: Knit to the end of the row.
Starting with a purl row, work 3 rows in SS.
Cast off.

Making up

Check the diagram on page 26 for measurements before sewing your animal together to ensure the clothes will fit comfortably.

Using matching yarn colours, sew up and stuff the body and head following the instructions on page 30. Pin the eye pieces in place so that they rest on the nose, as shown in the photographs. Sew in place using black yarn. Sew the eyes and nose in place following the instructions on page 30. Using black 4-ply (fingering) yarn, embroider the mouth using straight stitches.

Taking an ear, fold in half and sew the cast-on and cast-off edges together. Sew the small side seams. Pin in place on the sides of the head, using the photographs for guidance. When you are happy with their placement, sew in place. Pin the head to the body and sew firmly in place.

Sew up and stuff the arms and legs, and then sew them to the body following the instructions on page 30.

Fold the tail in half and sew the cast-on and cast-off edges together. Sew the small side seams. Sew the tail in place on the back of the body approximately 2.5cm (1in) from the bottom seam.

PANDA MINI-ME

Instructions

Legs and body

Using black aran (10-ply/worsted) yarn, cast on 5 sts and work as follows.

Next row: K2, M1, K1, M1, K2 (7 sts).

Next row: P1, P2tog, P1, P2togtbl, P1 (5 sts).

Starting with a knit row, work 4 rows in SS.

Cast off 1 st at the beginning of the next 2 rows (3 sts)*.

Break yarn and leave sts on a spare needle or stitch holder.

Make a second leg by working from the beginning of the instructions to *.

Place both legs on the needle with RS facing, change to white yarn and cast on 3 sts.

Knit these 3 sts, K2 from first leg, M1, K2tog (last st from the first leg and the first stitch from the second leg), M1, K2 (10 sts).

Next row: Cast on 3 sts, P5, M1, P3, M1, P5 (15 sts).

Starting with a knit row, work 4 rows in SS.

Next row: K2, ssK, K7, K2tog, K2 (13 sts).

Purl 1 row.

Change to black aran (10-ply/worsted) yarn.

Next row: K2, ssK, K5, K2tog, K2 (11 sts).

Purl 1 row.

Next row: K1, (K2tog) five times (6 sts).

Thread yarn through sts, leaving a length for sewing up.

Head

The cast-on edge forms the nose.

Using white yarn, cast on 4 sts.

Next row: (K1, M1) three times, K1 (7 sts).

Purl 1 row.

Cut a length of black aran (10-ply/worsted) yarn (approx. 50cm/19¾in) and work the sts on the following 2 rows with 'B' after them in black yarn and all other sts in white yarn, carrying the yarn across the back of the work.

Next row: K1, M1, K1, K1B, M1B, K1, M1B, K1B, K1, M1, K1 (11 sts).

Next row: P3, P2B, P1, P2B, P3.

Next row: K5, M1, K1, M1, K5 (13 sts).

Purl 1 row.

Next row: (K1, K2tog) four times, K1 (9 sts).

Purl 1 row.

Next row: (K2tog) four times, K1 (5 sts).

Thread yarn through remaining sts and fasten, leaving a length of yarn for sewing up.

MATERIALS

- Small amount of fluffy aran (10-ply/worsted) yarn in black
- Small amount of fluffy aran (10-ply/worsted) yarn in white
- Small amount of 4-ply (fingering) yarn in black
- Two 4mm beads
- Toy stuffing
- Black sewing thread

TOOLS

- 3.75mm (UK 9, US 5) DPN
- Sewing needle
- Stitch holder or spare knitting needle

Arm (make two)

Using black aran (10-ply/worsted) yarn, follow the instructions on page 31 for the Bunny Mini-me.

Ear (make two)

Using black aran (10-ply/worsted) yarn, cast on 1 st.

Next row: Kfbf (3 sts).

Starting with a purl row, work 5 rows in SS.

Next row: K3tog (1 st)

Thread yarn through remaining st and fasten, leaving a length of yarn for sewing up.

Making up

Matching yarn colours, sew up and stuff the legs and body following the instructions on page 32.

Sew up and stuff the head following the instructions on page 32. Fold an ear in half and sew around the edges. Repeat for the second ear. Pin the ears in place with the folded edge on the outside and sew securely in place.

Taking a sewing needle and black cotton, sew each bead in place for the eyes.

Using black 4-ply (fingering) yarn, embroider the nose using straight stitches. Sew the head firmly to the body.

Follow the instructions on page 32 to sew the arms and legs in place.

TEDDY BEAR

Instructions

Body

Using beige yarn and 3.75mm (UK 9, US 5) knitting needles, cast on 18 sts and purl 1 row.
Next row: K5, M1, K8, M1, K5 (20 sts).
Next row: P5, M1, P10, M1, P5 (22 sts).
Next row: K6, M1, K10, M1, K6 (24 sts).
Next row: P6, M1, P12, M1, P6 (26 sts).
Next row: K7, M1, K12, M1, K7 (28 sts).
Next row: P7, M1, P14, M1, P7 (30 sts).
Next row: K8, M1, K14, M1, K8 (32 sts).
Next row: P8, M1, P16, M1, P8 (34 sts).
Starting with a knit row, work 12 rows in SS.
Next row: K8, ssK, K14, K2tog, K8 (32 sts).
Purl 1 row.
Next row: K7, ssK, K14, K2tog, K7 (30 sts).
Purl 1 row.
Next row: K5, (ssK) twice, K12, (K2tog), twice, K5 (26 sts).
Next row: P4, (P2tog) twice, P10, (P2togtbl), twice, P4 (22 sts).
Next row: K3, (ssK) twice, K8, (K2tog), twice, K3 (18 sts).
Purl 1 row.
Cast off.

Head

Using beige yarn and 3.75mm (UK 9, US 5) knitting needles, cast on 8 sts and purl 1 row.
Next row: (K1, M1) seven times, K1 (15 sts).
Starting with a purl row, work 3 rows in SS.
Cast off and, with RS facing, pick up and knit 15 sts.
Purl 1 row.
Next row: K3, (Kfb) nine times, K3 (24 sts).
Purl 1 row.
Next row: (K8, M1) twice, K8 (26 sts).
Purl 1 row.
Next row: K1, M1, (K8, M1) three times, K1 (30 sts).
Purl 1 row.
Next row: K1, M1, K9, M1, K10, M1, K9, M1, K1 (34 sts).
Starting with a purl row, work 3 rows in SS.
Next row: (K3, K2tog) six times, K4 (28 sts).
Purl 1 row.
Next row: (K2, K2tog) seven times (21 sts).
Purl 1 row.

MATERIALS
- 60m (66yd) tweed (10-ply/worsted) yarn in beige
- Small amount of 4-ply (fingering) yarn in black
- Toy stuffing
- Two 6mm beads
- Black sewing thread

TOOLS:
- Two 3.75mm (UK 9, US 5) knitting needles and a spare needle for three-needle cast-off
- 2.75mm (UK 12, US 2) knitting needles
- Sewing needle

Next row: (K1, K2tog) seven times (14 sts).
Purl 1 row.
Thread yarn through remaining sts and leave a length for sewing up.

Leg (make two)

Using beige yarn, follow the instructions on page 28 for the Bunny.

Arm (make two)

Using beige yarn, follow the instructions on page 28 for the Bunny.

Ear (make two)

Using beige yarn and 3.75mm (UK 9, US 5) knitting needles, cast on 5 sts and, starting with a knit row, work 2 rows in SS.
Next row: K4, w&t (see page 14).
Next row: P3, w&t.
Next row: K3, w&t.
Next row: P3, w&t.
Next row: Knit to the end of the row.
Starting with a purl row, work 3 rows in SS.
Cast off.

Nose

Using black yarn and 2.75mm (UK 12, US 2) knitting needles, cast on 4 sts and, starting with a knit row, work 3 rows in SS.
Next row: (P2tog) twice (2 sts).
Thread yarn through remaining stitches, leaving a length of yarn for sewing up.

Tail

Using beige yarn and 3.75mm (UK 9, US 5) knitting needles, cast on 4 sts and, starting with a knit row, work 2 rows in SS.

Next row: K3, w&t.
Next row: P2, w&t.
Next row: Knit to the end of the row.
Starting with a purl row, work 3 rows in SS.
Cast off.

Making up

Check the diagram on page 26 for measurements before sewing your animal together to ensure the clothes will fit comfortably.

Sew up and stuff the body and head following the instructions on page 30. Sew the eyes and nose in place following the instructions on page 30. Using black yarn, embroider the mouth using straight stitches.

Taking an ear, fold in half and sew the cast-on and cast-off edges together. Sew the small side seams. Pin in place on the sides of the head, using the photographs for guidance. When you are happy with their placement, sew in place. Pin the head to the body and sew firmly in place.

Sew up and stuff the arms and legs, and then sew them to the body following the instructions on page 30.

Fold the tail in half and sew the cast-on and cast-off edges together. Sew the small side seams. Sew the tail in place on the back of the body approximately 2.5cm (1in) from the bottom seam.

TEDDY BEAR MINI-ME

Instructions

Legs and body

Using beige yarn, follow the instructions on page 31 for the Bunny Mini-me.

Head

The cast-on edge forms the nose.
Using beige yarn, follow the instructions on page 31 for the Bunny Mini-me.

Arm (make two)

Using beige yarn, follow the instructions on page 31 for the Bunny Mini-me.

Ear (make two)

Using beige yarn, cast on 1 st.
Next row: Kfbf (3 sts).
Starting with a purl row, work 5 rows in SS.
Next row: K3tog (1 st)
Thread yarn through remaining st and fasten, leaving a length of yarn for sewing up.

MATERIALS

- Small amount of aran (10-ply/worsted) yarn in beige
- Small amount of 4-ply (fingering) yarn in black
- Two 4mm beads
- Toy stuffing
- Black sewing thread

TOOLS

- 3.75mm (UK 9, US 5) DPN
- Sewing needle
- Stitch holder or spare knitting needle

Making up

Sew up and stuff the legs and body following the instructions on page 32. Sew up and stuff the head following the instructions on page 32.

Fold an ear in half and sew around the edges. Repeat for the second ear. Pin the ears in place with the folded edge on the outside and sew securely in place.

Taking a sewing needle and black cotton, sew each bead in place for the eyes, using the photograph for guidance.

Using black yarn, embroider the nose using straight stitches. Sew the head firmly to the body.

Follow the instructions on page 32 to sew the arms and legs in place.

DRESS ME!

Once you have made your animal, it's time to make him or her some clothes! All the clothes are interchangeable so you can make any clothes to fit any animal. There are five wardrobes to make: Off to School, On the Beach, Picnic Time, In the Snow and And so to Bed – so take your pick. There are lots of opportunities for your little ones to dress up their animals... and don't forget to make your Mini-me some accessories too (see pages 132–137)!

Some items of clothing are used in more than one wardrobe, and the second page of each section refers you to the correct page for the instructions to make your chosen item.

Happy knitting and sewing!

Time to make us some clothes!

OFF TO SCHOOL

page 75

page 65

page 71

page 62

page 63

page 76

page 60

page 68

page 64

page 74

RAGLAN CARDIGAN

MATERIALS
- 45m (49yd) of 4-ply (fingering) yarn in dark brown
- Three 10mm buttons

TOOLS
- 2.75mm (UK 12, US 2) and 3mm (UK 11, US 2/3) knitting needles
- Stitch markers
- Length of contrast yarn to hold sleeve stitches
- Sewing needle

TENSION (GAUGE)
- 8 sts = 2.5cm (1in) in SS using 3mm (UK 11, US 2/3) knitting needles

Instructions

Using 2.75mm (UK 12, US 2) knitting needles, cast on 44 sts and work as follows.

Next row: (K1, P1) to end of row.

Repeat last row twice more.

Next row: Working in K1, P1 rib and at the same time place markers as follows:

After 6th, 16th, 29th and 38th stitches.

Change to 3mm (UK 11, US 2/3) knitting needles.

Next row: (K to 1st before M, M1, K1, SM, K1, M1) four times, knit to end of row (52 sts).

Purl 1 row.

Repeat last two rows seven more times (108 sts).

Remove markers and divide for sleeves as follows, placing the fronts, back and one sleeve on a length of yarn as follows:

14 front sts, 26 sleeve sts, 28 back sts, 26 sleeve sts, 14 front sts.

With WS facing and starting with one set of 26 sleeve sts, cast on 2 sts at the beginning of the next two rows (30 sts).

Starting with a P row, work 2 rows in SS.

Change to 2.75mm (UK 12, US 2) knitting needles and work 4 rows in K1, P1 rib.

Cast off.

Repeat for second sleeve.

Slide all the body sts onto your needle and, starting with a purl row and using 3mm (UK 11, US 2/3) knitting needles, work across the body of the cardigan as follows:

P14 front sts, cast on 4 sts, P28 back sts, cast on 4 sts, P14 front sts (64 sts).

Continuing in SS work 6 rows in SS.

Change to 2.75mm (UK 12, US 2) knitting needles and work 4 rows in K1, P1 rib.

Cast off.

Button band

With RS facing, and using 2.75mm (UK 12, US 2) knitting needles pick up and knit 21 sts along the front edge of the cardigan.

Next row: (K1, P1) to last st, K1.

Next row: (P1, K1) to last st, P1.

Repeat last two rows once more. Cast off in rib.

Buttonhole band

With RS facing, and using 2.75mm (UK 12, US 2) knitting needles pick up and knit 21 sts along the front edge of the cardigan.

Next row: (K1, P1) to last st, K1.

Next row: (P1, K1) to last st, P1.

Next row: K1, P1, K2tog, YO, (K1, P1) three times, K2tog, YO, (K1, P1) twice, K1, K2tog, YO, P1, K1.

Next row: (P1, K1) to last st, P1.

Cast off in rib.

Making up

Lightly press and sew one of the sleeve seams together, matching the cast on stitches under the armhole to the cast on stitches on the body of the cardigan. Repeat for other sleeve. Sew in ends of yarn and sew the buttons to the buttonband using matching yarn.

TANK TOP

Instructions

Front

Using 2.75mm (UK 12, US 2) knitting needles, cast on 30 sts and work as follows.

Next row: (K1, P1) to end of row.

Repeat last row three more times.

Change to 3mm (UK 11, US 2/3) knitting needles.

Starting with a knit row, work 10 rows in SS.

Cast off 2 sts at the beginning of the next two rows (26 sts)*.

Next row: K10, K2tog, K1, turn, leaving the remaining 13 sts on a spare needle or stitch holder.

Working only over these 12 sts purl 1 row.

Next row: K to last 3 sts, K2tog, K1 (11 sts).

Purl 1 row.

Repeat last 2 rows six more times (5 sts).

Cast off.

With RS facing, rejoin yarn to remaining 13 sts and work as follows:

Next row: K1, ssK, K to end of row (12 sts).

Purl 1 row.

Repeat last 2 rows seven more times (5 sts).

Cast off.

Back

Work as for Front to *.

Starting with a knit row, work 12 rows in SS.

Next row: K8, cast off 10 sts, K7 (leaving two groups of 8 sts).

Working only over the first set of 8 sts, purl 1 row.

MATERIALS

- 38m (42yd) of 4-ply (fingering) yarn in dark brown

TOOLS

- 2.75mm (UK 12, US 2) and 3mm (UK 11, US 2/3) knitting needles
- Stitch marker
- Sewing needle

TENSION (GAUGE)

- 8 sts = 2.5cm (1in) on 3mm (UK 11, US 2/3) knitting needles

Next row: Cast off 3 sts, K to end of row (5 sts).

Purl 1 row.

Cast off.

With WS facing, rejoin yarn to remaining sts,

Next row: Cast off 3 sts, P to end of row (5 sts).

Starting with a knit row, work 2 rows in SS.

Cast off.

Making up

Join right shoulder seam.

With RS facing and 2.75mm (UK 12, US 2) knitting needles, pick up and knit 15 sts along front left neck edge, 1 st in centre of front neck, 15 sts along right front neck edge, and 15 sts along back neck edge (46 sts).

Place a stitch marker on the centre front neck stitch.

Next row: (K1, P1) to last st, K1.

Next row: Rib to 2 sts before marked st, ssK, K1, K2tog, rib to end of row.

Next row: Rib to 2 sts before marked st, K2tog, P1, ssK, rib to end of row.

Cast off in rib.

Join left shoulder seam.

With RS facing and using 2.75mm (UK 12, US 2) knitting needles, pick up and knit 15 sts along front armhole edge and 15 sts along back armhole edge (30 sts).

Next row: (K1, P1) to end of row.

Repeat last row twice more.

Cast off in rib.

Repeal for second armhole.

Join side seams and weave in all loose ends.

LACE-UP SHOES

MATERIALS
- 20m (22yd) of 4-ply (fingering) yarn in black (or cream and blue for sports shoes)
- Black (or cream) embroidery thread

TOOLS
- 2.75mm (UK 12, US 2) and 3mm (UK 11, US 2/3) knitting needles
- Sewing needle

TENSION (GAUGE)
- 8 sts = 2.5cm (1in) on 3mm (UK 11, US 2/3) knitting needles

Instructions

Sole (make two)

Using 3mm (UK 11, US 2/3) knitting needles and MC, cast on 4 sts and knit 1 row.
Next row: K1, M1, K to last st, M1, K1 (6 sts).
Knit 1 row.
Repeat the last 2 rows three more times (12 sts).
Knit 6 rows.
Next row: K1, K2tog, K to last 3 sts, K2tog, K1 (10 sts).
Knit 1 row.
Repeat the last 2 rows twice more (6 sts).
Next row: K1, (K2tog) twice, K1 (4 sts).
Cast off.

Top (make two)

Using 2.75mm (UK 12, US 2) knitting needles and MC cast on 32 sts and knit 3 rows.
Change to 3mm (UK 11, US 2/3) knitting needles and CC yarn.
Starting with a knit row, work 2 rows in st st.
Next row: K10, (ssK) twice, K4, (K2tog) twice, K10 (28 sts).
Next row: P10, P2tog, P4, P2togtbl, P10 (26 sts).
Next row: K9, ssK, K4, K2tog, K9 (24 sts).
Next row: P8, P2tog, P4, P2togtbl, P8 (22 sts).
Change to 2.75mm (UK 12, US 2) knitting needles and CC, knit 2 rows.
Cast off loosely.

Making up

Taking one of the tops, sew the back seam together. Pin in place onto the sole and carefully sew around the edge. Cut a length of embroidery thread approximately 30cm (11¾in) long. Thread through the front of the shoe to look like laces, using the photograph for guidance. Make a bow, trim the thread and knot each end to prevent fraying. Repeat for the second shoe.

MARY JANES

MATERIALS
- 20m (22yd) of 4-ply (fingering) yarn in black
- Two 8mm black buttons

TOOLS
- 2.75mm (UK 12, US 2) and 3mm (UK 11, US 2/3) knitting needles
- Sewing needle

TENSION (GAUGE)
- 8 sts = 2.5cm (1in)

Instructions

Sole (make two)

Using 3mm (UK 11, US 2/3) knitting needles, cast on 4 sts and knit 1 row.
Next row: K1, M1, K to last st, M1, K1 (6 sts).
Knit 1 row.
Repeat the last 2 rows three more times (12 sts).
Knit 6 rows.
Next row: K1, K2tog, K to last 3 sts, K2tog, K1 (10 sts).
Knit 1 row.
Repeat the last two rows twice more (6 sts).
Next row: K1, (K2tog) twice, K1 (4 sts).
Cast off.

Top (make two)

Using 2.75mm (UK 12, US 2) knitting needles, cast on 32 sts and knit 3 rows.
Change to 3mm (UK 11, US 2/3) knitting needles.
Next row: P10, (P2tog) twice, P4, (P2togtbl) twice, P10 (28 sts).
Next row: K10, SSK, K4, K2tog, K10 (26 sts).
Next row: P9, P2tog, P4, P2togtbl, P9 (24 sts).
Cast off.

Strap (make two)

Using 3mm (UK 11, US 2/3) knitting needles, cast on 12 sts and knit 2 rows.
Cast off.

Making up

Taking one of the tops, sew the back seam together. Pin in place onto the sole and carefully sew around the edge. Pin one end of the strap in place under the inside edge of the shoe and the other on the top of the shoe on the outside edge. Sew the strap in place on the inside edge. Sew a button in place on the other end of the strap, securing the strap at the same time and using the photograph for guidance. Repeat for the second shoe.

SHIRTS & TOPS

I used an old school shirt to make this.

MATERIALS

- A small amount of school shirt, patterned or pyjama fabric
- Three 8mm buttons to match fabric
- Thread to match fabric
- Three snap fasteners

TOOLS

- Sewing machine or sewing needle

SIZE

- Approx. 10.5cm (4¹⁄₈in) wide

Instructions

The shirts and pyjama tops in this book are all made using these instructions. To make the boy's pyjama top (page 119), cut out templates on pages 142–143. You will need: 1 x shirt back, 2 x shirt front (1 in reverse), 2 x shirt sleeve, 2 x pyjama collar (1 in reverse). To make the boy's pyjama top, follow the instructions for the shirt, using the pyjama collar pieces instead of the shirt collar.

To make the girl's pyjama top (page 119), you will need: 1 x shirt back, 2 x pyjama front (1 in reverse) and 2 x shirt sleeve. You will also need 1m (39½in) of trim to edge the sleeves and neckline. Sew the trim in place to the RS of the fabric and fold the edge back so that the trim shows. Sew the trim to the neckline after step 6.

1 Cut out the fabric using the templates on pages 142–143. You will need: 1 x shirt back, 2 x shirt sleeve, 2 x shirt front (1 cut in reverse) and 2 x shirt collar (1 cut in reverse).

2 Thread your sewing machine with matching thread and refer to page 11 for settings to use for stitch length and width.

3 Neaten the edges of the back, two front pieces and two arm pieces with a narrow zigzag stitch.

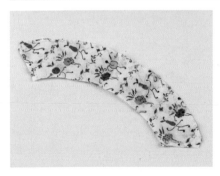 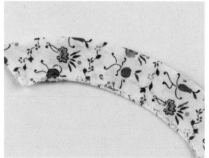 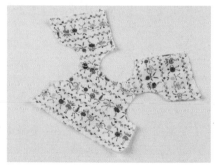

4 Zigzag around the side and top edges of each collar piece. Place with RS together and, using a straight stitch, sew around the side and top edges to join. Trim the seam allowance a little and cut diagonally across the two sewn corners.

5 Turn through, being careful with the corners, and press flat. Join the lower edge of the collar by zigzagging the two edges together. Set aside.

6 With RS together, pin the two front sections to the back and sew across the shoulder seams. Press the seams open.

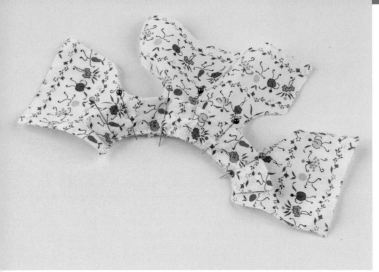

7 With RS together, pin the collar in place as follows. Fold the collar in half and, with the RS of the shirt back facing, pin the centre of the collar to the centre of the back. Then ease each side of the collar to fit round the neckline and pin. Tack in place before sewing, if necessary.

8 Machine stitch the collar in place close to the fabric edge using a straight stitch.

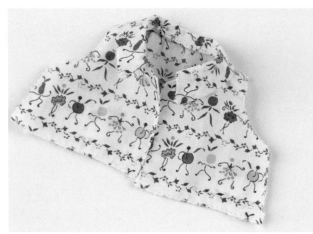

9 Fold the inside edge of the collar to the inside of the shirt and machine in place close to the collar seam using a straight stitch. Press.

10 Fold in half and mark the centre of the sleeve with a pin. Match the centre of the sleeve to the shoulder seam, with RS together. Pin the rest of the sleeve in place, easing it round the armhole as you go. Tack in place before sewing, if necessary.

11 Machine stitch in place. Repeat for the second sleeve. Press the seam towards the body.

12 Press the edge of each sleeve under by 5mm (¼in) and machine stitch close to the edge.

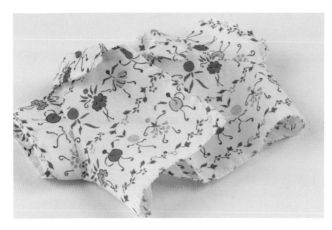

13 Pin the side seams with RS together and machine stitch together. Press seams flat.

14 Press the front edges of the shirt in by 5mm (¼in) and machine sew close to the edge.

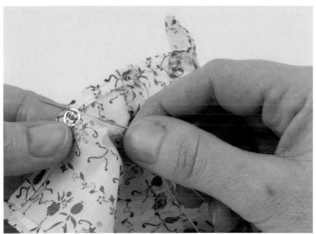

15 Then sew on three snap fasteners, making sure they are evenly spaced.

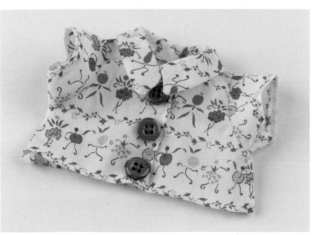

16 Finally, sew on the buttons to correspond with each snap fastener. This part is a bit fiddly, as you need to make sure that the cotton does not cross the snap fastener underneath. Wrap the thread around the stitches underneath the button once or twice as you go to keep the stitches tight.

TROUSERS & SHORTS

Instructions

These instructions are used to make all the trousers, shorts and pyjama bottoms included in the book. Use them to make the school trousers, jeans (page 105), the girl's pyjama shorts and the boy's pyjama trousers (page 119), and the frog and sailboat shorts (page 89).

To make the school trousers and the boy's pyjama trousers, cut out the template on page 140 using the relevant fabric. You will need 2 x trouser pieces (and one small button for the school trousers. I re-used the button from my daughter's school trousers). Then follow steps 1–3, 8–10 and 12–16.

To make the shorts and girl's pyjama shorts, cut out the template on page 140. You will need 2 x shorts pieces. For the pyjama shorts you will also need 50cm (19¾in) of trim to edge the legs of the shorts. This is added when you neaten the edges at step 3 by sewing to the RS of the fabric and folding this edge towards the inside. For all the shorts follow steps 1–3, 8–10 and 12–16.

Follow all the steps here to make the jeans.

1 Cut out the fabric using the template on page 140.

2 Thread your sewing machine with matching thread and see page 11 for settings to use for stitch length and width.

3 Neaten the edges by zigzagging all the way round.

4 Press the legs in half with WS together to make a visible crease line. Stitch down the centre line with orange thread.

5 Using the guide markings on the template, tack a curved running stitch for the pockets on both pieces of fabric in contrast thread.

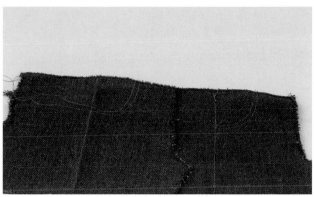

6 Using the tacking line as a guide, sew round using a straight stitch on one side to denote the pockets. Remove the tacking thread and sew the second line.

7 Leave a long thread so you can take it through to the back and fasten it off.

8 Pin the leg pieces with RS together and, using straight stitch, sew the leg seam for both pieces of fabric. Press the leg seams open.

9 Turn one leg through to the RS and slide it inside the other leg, so that the RS are together, matching seam edges and notches together. Pin in place. The two pins on the right-hand side mark where the notches are for the tail opening.

10 Starting at the un-notched side (the front edge), sew around the seam using a straight stitch, leaving the section between the notches unsewn (this will form the tail opening).

11 Press the top part of the seam open and turn through. The seam is now complete, with an opening for the tail. Tack the fly in place, then sew using orange thread.

12 Press a 5mm (¼in) seam allowance into the end of the trouser legs and pin. Machine sew carefully on the inside edge using orange thread. Repeat for the second leg.

13 Press a 1cm (³⁄₈in) seam allowance into the waistband of the trousers. Starting 1cm (³⁄₈in) to the right of the back seam, sew the waistband, stopping 1cm (³⁄₈in) before the back seam. This leaves a gap through which to thread the elastic. Leave a long thread to hand sew once the elastic has been inserted (not pictured).

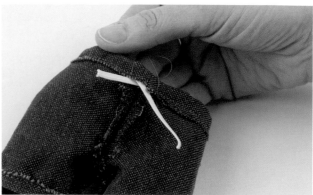

14 Thread the elastic onto a darning needle or bodkin, push the needle into the seam and thread the elastic through, bringing it out of the other side of the seam.

15 Tighten the elastic, gathering the fabric as you go until it fits your animal's waist, then tie a knot in the elastic. Trim the ends of the elastic then slide the knot into the seam. Take the tail end of the orange thread that you left in step 13 and hand sew the gap in the seam closed.

16 Finally, using running stitch, hand sew around the tail opening at the back of the trousers.

Note:
Please note that the top stitching for the side seams and pockets, shown in steps 4–7 and 11, is only used when making the jeans.

FABRIC DRESS

These instructions are used to make the school dress (page 59) and also the patterned fabric dress (page 93), which has a matching fabric (rather than felt) collar.

I used an old school dress to make this.

MATERIALS
- Small amount of school dress or patterned fabric
- Small amount of white felt (for school dress)
- Three small buttons
- Sewing thread to match fabric

TOOLS
- Sewing machine or sewing needle

SIZE
- Approx. 13.5cm (5¼in) long

Note:

If you are making the patterned fabric dress (see page 78), use the template on page 141 for the collar and follow steps 4–5 on page 65 and 7–9 on page 66 for the shirt collar.

Instructions

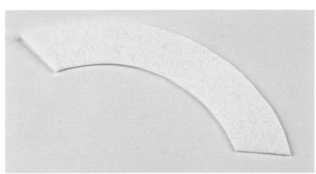

1 Using the template for the school dress collar on page 141, cut out one collar piece in white felt. Cut out the fabric pieces using the templates on pages 138, 141 and 142. You will need: 1 x dress back, 2 x dress sleeve (1 cut in reverse), 2 x dress front (1 cut in reverse) and 1 x skirt piece. (You will also need 2 x shirt collar pieces – 1 cut in reverse – if you are making the patterned fabric dress.) Neaten the edges of all the fabric pieces, following steps 1–3 on page 65 for the school shirt.

School dress collar

Patterned fabric dress collar

2 Using a contrasting colour that matches the dress fabric, topstitch all the way round approximately 3mm (¹/₈in) from the outside edge.

3 Set the collar aside and follow steps 6–13 for the shirt on pages 65–67 (the collar will be attached in step 7 of the shirt instructions).

4 Sew a zigzag stitch around the edge of the skirt fabric.

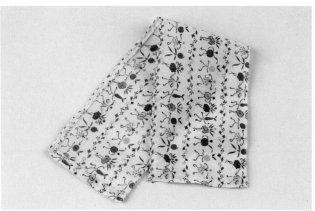

5 Press a seam of 5mm (¼in) at each short edge and one long edge and machine sew each one using straight stitch.

6 The other long edge will form the top of the skirt section. Using a long straight stitch (I used a stitch length of 4.5), machine sew two lines along the top edge, leaving long threads that you will use to gather the skirt.

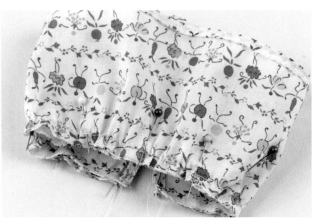

7 Evenly gather the skirt and with RS together, pin the gathered edge of the skirt to the lower edge of the bodice, ensuring that the gathers are evenly distributed and matching the edges of the skirt to the edges of the bodice. Then machine stitch the two pieces together. Tack in place before sewing, if necessary.

8 Press the seam towards the bodice and hand sew over each end of the seam to keep it in place.

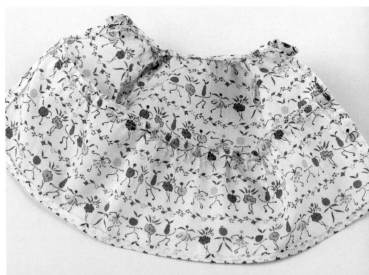

9 Then sew on three snap fasteners, making sure they are evenly spaced.

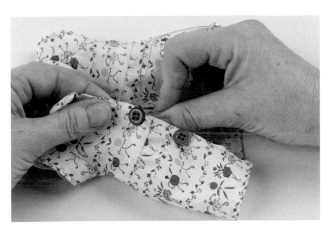

10 Finally, sew on the buttons to correspond with each snap fastener. This part is a bit fiddly, as you need to make sure that the cotton does not cross the press stud underneath. Wrap the thread around the stitches underneath the button once or twice as you go to keep the stitches tight.

Top tip!

If you pin the seams vertically instead of horizontally, you can leave the pins in while you machine stitch. Be careful as the needle approaches the pins, though!

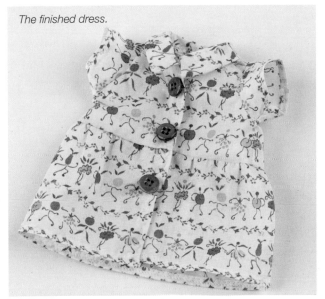

The finished dress.

FELT BOOK

Instructions

1 Cut out one book cover and two inside covers in your chosen felt colour using the templates on page 141. Using brown/grey felt, cut out your chosen animal face.

2 Fold the book cover in half and place the animal face so that it is central on the front cover. Sew carefully in place using matching thread.

3 Using black embroidery thread, embroider the features onto the bear or bunny, as shown in the photographs below.

4 Place one inside cover piece on top of the cover with three edges against the outside edges of the cover. Sew the two pieces together by overstitching them around the three outside edges, leaving the inside edge open. This will leave a small vertical gap in the middle of the inside cover. Repeat for the second inside cover.

5 Fold the book in half with the cover showing and sew a line of stitches from the top edge of the spine of the book to the bottom using matching thread.

the templates on page 141

MATERIALS
- Small amount of blue or green felt and some brown or grey felt
- Sewing thread to match
- Black embroidery thread
- Piece of paper 210 x 297mm (8¼ x 11¾in)
- Glue

TOOLS
- Sewing needle

SIZE
- Approx. 4.5 x 5.5cm (1¾ x 2⅛in)

6 To make some pages for the book, take a piece of paper 210 x 297mm (8¼ x 11¾in) in size and cut out a section lengthwise that is 5cm (2in) high. Fold the piece in a concertina to make pages 4cm (1½in) wide. Using some glue, stick two pages together, back to back. Repeat for the other pages. Thread the first and last pages into the inside covers to form a book.

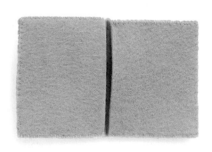

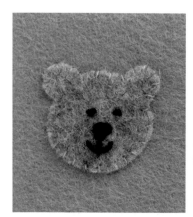

HAIRBAND

Instructions

Flower

Cast on 21 sts and work as follows:
Next row: (sl1, K3) five times, sl1.
Next row: (sl1, P3) five times, sl1.
Next row: (K1, sl1, K2tog, psso) five times, K1 (11 sts).
Next row: (P2tog) five times, P1 (6 sts).
Thread yarn through remaining sts, leaving a length of yarn for sewing up.

Making up

Gather remaining stitches and secure, then sew the small side seam. Using embroidery thread and needle, sew a few French knots (see page 21) for the centre of the flower and a few straight stitches to add definition. Sew the flower securely to the elastic hairband.

SATCHEL

MATERIALS
- Small amount of brown felt
- Small piece of white card
- Sewing thread to match felt

TOOLS
- Sewing needle

SIZE
- Approx. 8cm (3¹/₈in) wide

Instructions

1 Cut the pieces for the satchel out of brown felt, using the templates opposite.

2 Taking the front satchel piece and the name tag holder, pin the holder in place on the middle of the front, using the

dotted lines on the template for guidance. Sew the holder in place along the side and bottom edges.

3 Taking a strap holder, fold in half lengthwise, overlapping by 5mm (¼in) and sew the two edges together to make a 'loop'. Repeat for the second strap holder. Pin each strap holder in place either side of the name tag holder, using the dotted lines on the template for guidance. Sew in place.

4 Taking the front piece and the satchel gusset, pin the gusset in place around the curved edge of the front piece. Oversew using matching sewing thread and a sewing needle.

5 Pin the other side of the gusset to the back of the satchel, making sure the gusset is even on both sides. Sew in place.

6 Oversew around the edges of the straps and handle to strengthen them.

7 Now you have the body of the satchel sewn together, pin the straps in place so that the larger ends are on the front flap of the satchel and the smaller ends are pointing downwards through the strap loop.

8 Sew each end of the handle to the top edge of the satchel, as shown in the photograph.

9 Cut a small piece of white card to fit inside the name tag holder.

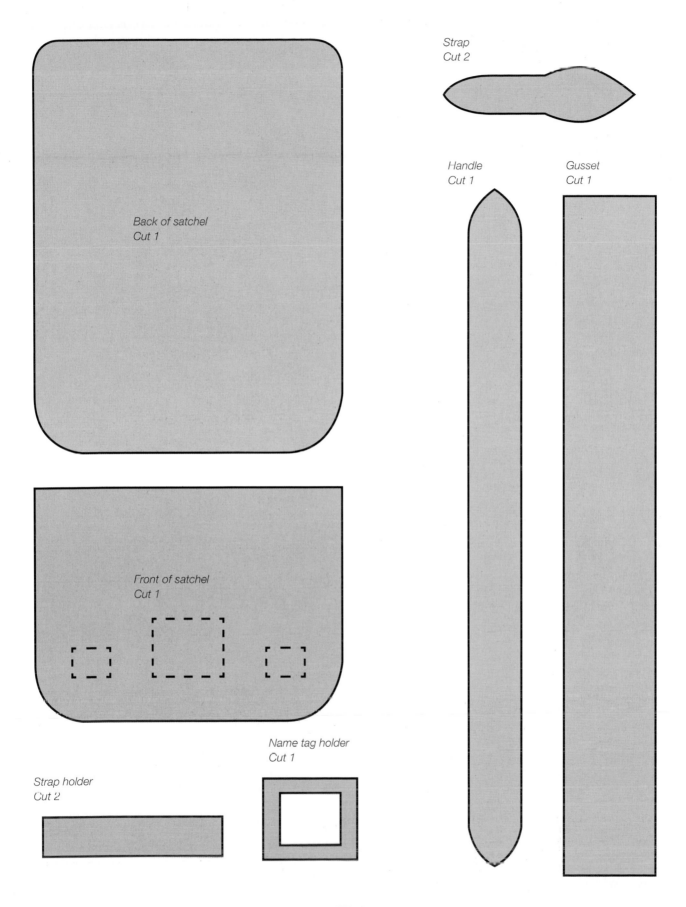

Back of satchel
Cut 1

Front of satchel
Cut 1

Strap holder
Cut 2

Name tag holder
Cut 1

Strap
Cut 2

Handle
Cut 1

Gusset
Cut 1

ON THE BEACH

page 80

page 89

page 90

page 87

page 82

page 84

page 90

page 89

page 85

page 86

page 88

T-SHIRT

Instructions

Front

Using 2.75mm (UK 12, US 2) knitting needles and CC, cast on 32 sts and knit 2 rows.
Change to 3mm (UK 11, US 2/3) knitting needles and MC.
Starting with a knit row, work 14 rows in SS.
Cast off 2 sts at the beginning of the next two rows (28 sts).
Next row: K1, ssK, K to last 3 sts, K2tog, K1 (26 sts)*.
Starting with a purl row, work 5 rows in st st.
Next row: K9, cast off 8 sts, K8 (leaving two groups of 9 sts).
Working over the first set of sts, purl 1 row.
Next row: K1, ssK, K6 (8 sts).
Purl 1 row.
Next row: K1, ssK, K5 (7 sts).
Purl 1 row.
Next row: K1, ssK, K4 (6 sts).
Purl 1 row.
Next row: K1, ssK, K3, (5 sts).
Purl 1 row.
Cast off.
With WS facing, rejoin yarn to remaining 9 sts and purl 1 row.
Next row: K6, K2tog, K1 (8 sts).
Purl 1 row.
Next row: K5, K2tog, K1 (7 sts).
Purl 1 row.
Next row: K4, K2tog, K1 (6 sts).
Purl 1 row.
Next row: K3, K2tog, K1 (5 sts).
Purl 1 row.
Cast off.

Back

Work as for Front to *.
Starting with a purl row, work 11 rows in st st.
Next row: K8, cast off 10 sts, K7 (leaving two groups of 8 sts).
Working over the first set of sts, purl 1 row.
Next row: Cast off 3 sts, K to end of row (5 sts).
Purl 1 row.
Cast off.
With RS facing, rejoin yarn to remaining 8 sts and knit 1 row.
Next row: Cast off 3 sts, P to end of row (5 sts).
Knit 1 row.
Cast off.

Neckband

Join right shoulder seam.
Using 2.75mm (UK 12, US 2) knitting needles and CC yarn.
With RS facing, pick up and knit 22 sts along the front neck edge and 18 sts along the back neck edge (40 sts).
Knit 2 rows.
Cast off.

Sleeves

Join left shoulder seam and start with one armhole.
With RS facing and using 3mm (UK 11, US 2/3) knitting needles and MC yarn, pick up and knit 26 sts around the armhole edge.
Starting with a purl row, work 5 rows in st st.
Change to 2.75mm (UK 12, US 2) knitting needles and CC yarn and knit 2 rows.
Cast off.
Repeat for second sleeve.

Pocket

Using 3mm (UK 11, US 2/3) knitting needles and MC yarn, cast on 8 sts and work in st st until work measures 2cm (¾in).
Change to 2.75mm (UK 12, US 2) knitting needles and CC yarn.
Knit 1 row.
Cast off.

Making up

Sew the sleeve and side seams. Pin the pocket in place, using the photograph for guidance. Sew in place using matching yarn colours.

SWIMSUIT

Front of swimsuit

MATERIALS
- 22m (24yd) of 4-ply (fingering) yarn in fuchsia pink (MC)
- 11m (12yd) of 4-ply (fingering) yarn in orange (CC)
- Two 10mm pink buttons

TOOLS
- 2.75mm (UK 12, US 2) and 3mm (UK 11, US 2/3) knitting needles
- Sewing needle

TENSION (GAUGE)
- 8 sts = 2.5cm (1in) on 3mm (UK 11, US 2/3) knitting needles

Instructions

Note:
The swimsuit is made in one piece, beginning at the front.

Using MC yarn and 3mm (UK 11, US 2/3) knitting needles, cast on 4 sts and, starting with a knit row, work 4 rows in SS.

Next row: K1, M1, K to last st, M1, K1 (6 sts).

Next row: P1, M1, P to last st, M1, P1 (8 sts).

Next row: K1, M1, K to last st, M1, K1 (10 sts).

Purl 1 row.

Cast on 3 sts at the beginning of the next 4 rows (22 sts).

Starting with a knit row, work 8 rows in SS.

**Join in CC. *Continuing in SS, work 2 rows.

Change to MC and work 4 rows in SS*.

Repeat this 6-row colour pattern once more (to make one more CC stripe working from * to *).

Change to 2.75mm (UK 12, US 2) knitting needles and CC yarn and knit 3 rows.

Cast off.**

With RS facing and using 3mm (UK 11, US 2/3) knitting needles and MC, pick up and knit 4 sts from cast-on edge of knitted piece.

Back of swimsuit showing the tail hole.

Next row: P1, M1, P to last st, M1, P1 (6 sts).
Cast on 2 sts at the beginning of the next 4 rows (14 sts).
Cast on 3 sts at the beginning of the next 2 rows (20 sts).
Next row: K1, M1, K7, cast off 4 sts, K6, M1, K1 (making two groups of 9 sts).
Next row: P9, (M1) four times, P9 (22 sts).
The last 2 rows form a hole for the tail to thread through.
Starting with a knit row, work 10 rows in SS.
Work as for Front from ** to **.

Leg edging

With RS facing, using 3mm (UK 11, US 2/3) knitting needles and CC yarn, pick up and knit 13 sts along the sloped leg edge to the centre bottom seam. Pick up and knit a further 13 sts along the second half of the leg edge (26 sts).
Knit 1 row.
Cast off.
Repeat for second leg edge.

Strap (make two)

Using 3mm (UK 11, US 2/3) knitting needles and CC yarn, cast on 21 sts and knit 2 rows.
Next row: K2, YO, K2tog, K to end of row (to create a buttonhole).
Knit 2 rows.
Cast off.

Making up

Sew the side seams of the swimsuit, matching colours as you sew. Pin the straps in place with the buttonholes on the back of the swimsuit and using the photographs for guidance. Sew the straps to the front of the swimsuit. Sew the buttons in place on the back of the swimsuit.

WAVY SKIRT

MATERIALS

- 30m (33yd) of 4-ply (fingering) sock yarn in multicoloured (MC)
- 8m (9yd) of 4-ply (fingering) yarn in pink (CC)

TOOLS

- 2.75mm (UK 12, US 2) and 3.25mm (UK 10, US 3) knitting needles
- Sewing needle

TENSION (GAUGE)

- 12 sts = 5cm (2in) over pattern using 3.25mm (UK 10, US 3) knitting needles

Instructions

Note:

The skirt is worked in one piece.

Using CC and 3.25mm (UK 10, US 3) knitting needles, cast on 72 sts and knit 2 rows.
Change to MC and work as follows:
Next row: ((K2tog) twice, (K1, YO) four times, (K2tog) twice), repeat six times.
Purl 1 row.
Repeat last two rows six more times.
Work pattern row once more.
Next row: P2, (P2tog, P4) eleven times, P2tog, P2 (60 sts).
Change to 2.75mm (UK 10, US 3) knitting needles and CC yarn, and knit 6 rows.
Cast off.

Making up

Sew in all loose ends of yarn and sew the side seam using matching yarn colours. Press gently with a steam iron.

BEACH BAG

MATERIALS

- 55m (60yd) of DK (8-ply/light worsted) cotton yarn in blue (MC)
- 45m (49yd) of DK (8-ply/light worsted) cotton yarn in cream (CC)
- Two bag handles cut in dark brown felt (see template on page 141)
- Four decorative buttons
- Dark brown sewing thread

TOOLS

- 3.25mm (UK 10, US 3) knitting needles
- Sewing needle

SIZE

- 6cm (2³/₈in) high (excluding handles)

Instructions

Top of bag

Using MC cast on 40 sts and knit 4 rows.
Join in CC yarn and knit 4 rows.
Change to MC and knit 6 rows.
Repeat last ten rows once more.
Cast off using MC.

Base

Using MC cast on 3 sts and knit 1 row.
Next row: (K1, M1) twice, K1 (5 sts).
Knit 1 row
Next row: K1, M1, K3, M1, K1 (7 sts).
Knit 18 rows.
Next row: (K1, K2tog) twice, K1 (5 sts).
Knit 1 row.
Next row: K2tog, K1, K2tog (3 sts).
Cast off.

Making up

Taking the main bag piece, carefully sew the side seam together. Pin the bag to the base, placing the seam halfway along one side. Sew in place using MC yarn.

Fold one of the felt bag handles in half lengthwise and oversew using matching sewing thread between the two markers. Repeat for the second handle. Pin the handles in place using the photograph for guidance. Using sewing thread and a sewing needle, sew each button in place, securing the handle to the bag at the same time.

BEACH TOWEL

MATERIALS

- 35m (38yd) of DK (8-ply/light worsted) cotton yarn in blue (MC)
- 25m (27yd) of DK (8-ply/light worsted) cotton yarn in cream (CC)

TOOLS

- 4mm (UK 8, US 6) knitting needles
- Sewing needle

SIZE

- 24 x 14cm (9½ x 5½in)

Instructions

Work in GS throughout.
Cast on 24 sts using MC.
Knit 2 rows in MC.
Join in CC and knit 2 rows.
Repeat the last 4 rows 19 more times, ending with CC.
Knit 2 rows in MC.
Cast off.

Making up

Weave in all loose ends and press lightly.

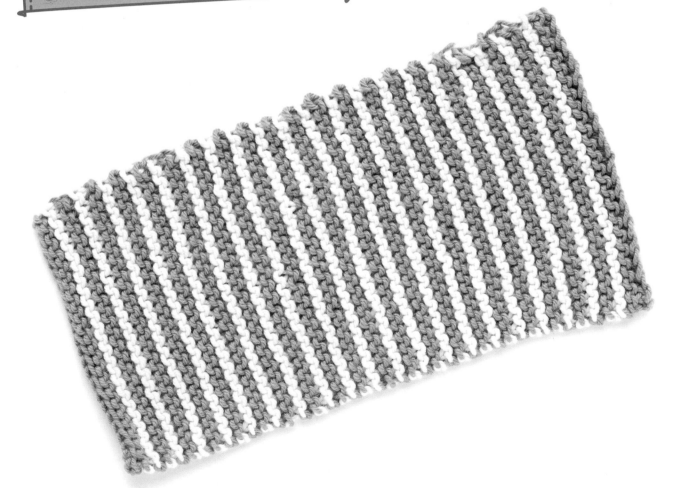

FELT TOP

MATERIALS
- Small amount of felt in the colour of your choice
- Small amount of variegated yarn
- Sewing thread to match fabric

TOOLS
- Sewing machine or sewing needle

SIZE
- Approx. 11cm (4¼in) wide across bottom edge

Instructions

1 Cut out the felt pieces using the templates on page 139. You will need: 1 x felt dress front and 2 x felt dress backs.

2 Follow steps 3–5 for the felt dress on pages 101 and 102.

3 Topstitch a line of stitches around the bottom edge of the felt top.

4 Follow steps 8 and 9 on page 102.

5 Make a flower using the instructions for the hairband on page 75 and sew in place.

HANDBAG

Instructions

Cast on 12 sts and work 4 rows in GS.
Next row: K1, M1, K to last st, M1, K1 (14 sts).
Knit 3 rows.
Next row: K1, M1, K to last st, M1, K1 (16 sts).
Knit 5 rows.
Next row: K1, ssK, K to last 3 sts, K2tog, K1 (14 sts).
Knit 3 rows.
Next row: K1, ssK, K to last 3 sts, K2tog, K1 (12 sts).
Knit 1 row.
Repeat last two rows once more (10 sts).
Next row: K1, M1, K to last st, M1, K1 (12 sts).
Knit 1 row.
Repeat last two rows once more (14 sts).
Knit 2 rows.
Next row: K1, M1, K to last 3 sts, M1, K1 (16 sts).
Knit 5 rows.
Next row: K1, ssK, K to last 3 sts, K2tog, K1 (14 sts).
Knit 3 rows.
Next row: K1, ssK, K to last 3 sts, K2tog, K1 (12 sts).
Knit 4 rows.
Next row: K1, ssK, K to last 3 sts, K2tog, K1 (10 sts).
Knit 8 rows.
Next row: K4, cast off 2 sts, K3 (leaving two groups of 4 sts).
Next row: K4, (M1) twice, K4 (10 sts).
Next row: K1, ssK, K to last 3 sts, K2tog, K1 (8 sts).
Repeat last row twice more (4 sts).
Cast off.

Handle

Cast on 4 sts and, using the i-cord technique (see page 33 under *Ear edging*), work in SS until strap measures 14cm (5½in).
Cast off.

Making up

Fold the front and back of the bag together and sew the side seams. Sew the button in place on the front of the bag. Sew each end of the handle to the top inside edge of the handbag. Weave in all loose ends.

SHORTS

Instructions

To make the Frog or the Sailboat shorts, cut out the Shorts template on page 140 and follow steps 1–3, 8–10 and 12–16 on pages 68–70 for the Trousers & Shorts.

Front of shorts

Back, showing hole for tail.

FLIP FLOPS

Instructions

1 Cut out all the pieces using the templates on page 139. You will need: 4 x felt soles, 2 x heavyweight interfacing soles, 2 x strap pieces and 2 x strap trim pieces in a contrasting colour.

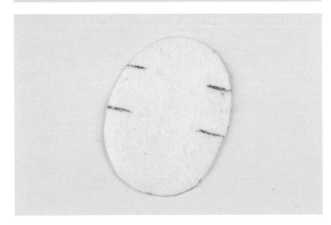

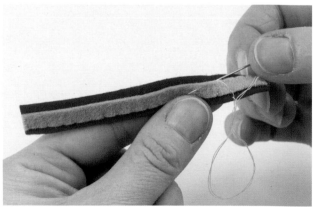

2 Trim the interfacing piece to make it 2–3mm (approximately $\frac{1}{8}$in) smaller than the felt pieces. Mark the strap position as shown on the template.

3 Hand stitch the light blue strap trim to the red strap using matching thread.

4 Layer up an interfacing piece between two felt soles. Insert one end of the strap by approximately 5mm (¼in) under the interfacing and stitch through the strap, taking the needle to the back through the strap piece and then bringing it to the front through all the layers, making sure it lines up with the marks on the sole lining.

5 Starting at the top right of the shoe, begin oversewing around the edge until you reach the strap mark on the interfacing.

6 The first side of the strap is now secure within the layers of fabric.

7 Continue sewing around and repeat for the other side of the strap.

8 Finally, stitch the button on in the centre or at the side of the strap.

PICNIC TIME

page 96

page 71

page 65

page 99

page 98

page 64

page 94

page 101

page 99

page 68

page 63

DRESS

Instructions

Front

Using MC and 3.25mm (UK 10, US 3) knitting needles, cast on 36 sts and knit 2 rows.
Change to CC yarn and work as follows:
Next row: ((K2tog) twice, (K1, YO) four times, (K2tog) twice) three times.
Purl 1 row.
Repeat last 2 rows nine more times.
Next row: K2, (K2tog, K4) five times, K2tog, K2 (30 sts).
Change to 3mm (UK 11, US 2/3) knitting needles and MC yarn, and purl 1 row.
Purl 1 row (on RS).
Next row: P1, P2tog, P to last 3 sts, P2tog, K1 (28 sts).
Starting with a knit row, work 8 rows in SS.
Cast off 2 sts at the beginning of the next 2 rows (24 sts).
Next row: K1, ssK, K to last 3 sts, K2tog, K1 (22 sts).
Purl 1 row*.
Shape neck as follows:
Next row: K7, cast off 8, K6 (leaving two groups of 7 sts).
Turn, and working over first set of 7 sts only, purl 1 row.
Next row: K1, ssK, K4 (6 sts).
Purl 1 row.
Next row: K1, ssK, K3 (5 sts).
Purl 1 row.
Next row: K1, ssK, K2 (4 sts).
Starting with a purl row, work 3 rows in SS.
Cast off.
With WS facing, rejoin MC yarn to remaining 7 sts and purl 1 row.
Next row: K4, K2tog, K1 (6 sts).
Purl 1 row.
Next row: K3, K2tog, K1 (5 sts).
Purl 1 row.
Next row, K2, K2tog, K1 (4 sts).
Starting with a purl row work 3 rows in SS.
Cast off.

Back

Work as for Front to *.
Continuing in SS, work 4 rows.
Next row: K5, cast off 12, K4 (leaving two groups of 5 sts).
Working over one set of 5 sts:

MATERIALS
- 25m (27yd) of 4-ply (fingering) yarn in purple (MC)
- 35m (38yd) of 4-ply (fingering) yarn in lilac (CC)

TOOLS
- 2.75mm (UK 12, US 2), 3mm (UK 11, US 2/3) and 3.25mm (UK 10, US 3) knitting needles
- Sewing needle

TENSION (GAUGE)
- 8 sts = 2.5cm (1in) worked on 3mm (UK 11, US 2/3) knitting needles

Purl 1 row.
Next row: K1, ssK, K2 (4 sts).
Starting with a purl row, work 3 rows in SS.
Cast off.
With WS facing rejoin MC yarn to remaining 5 sts and purl 1 row.
Next row: K2, K2tog, K1 (4 sts).
Starting with a purl row, work 3 rows in SS.
Cast off.

Neck edge

Join right shoulder seam.

With RS facing and using 2.75mm (UK 12, US 2) knitting needles and CC yarn, pick up and knit 21 sts along the front neck edge and 18 sts along the back neck edge (39 sts).

Knit 1 row.

Cast off using a picot cast-off as follows:

Cast off 2 sts, *sl st back to LH needle, cast on 2 sts, cast off 4 sts*.

Repeat from * to * to last st, cast off remaining st.

Sleeves

Join left shoulder seam and start with one armhole.

With RS facing and using 3mm (UK 11, US 2/3) knitting needles and MC yarn, pick up and knit 26 sts around the armhole edge.

Starting with a purl row, work 5 rows in SS.

Change to 2.75mm (UK 12, US 2) knitting needles and CC yarn.

Knit 2 rows.

Cast off using a picot cast-off as follows:

Cast off 2 sts, (sl st back to LH needle, cast on 2 sts, cast off 4 sts), repeat to last 2 sts, cast off last 2 sts.

Repeat for second sleeve.

Making up

Weave in all loose ends and sew the sleeve and side seams using matching yarn colours. Press gently with a steam iron.

 # BOLERO

Instructions

Back

Using 2.75mm (UK 12, US 2) knitting needles, cast on 28 sts and work as follows:

Next row: (K2, P2) repeat to end of row.

Repeat last row three more times to form rib edging.

Change to 3mm (UK 11, US 2/3) knitting needles and, starting with a knit row, work 8 rows in SS.

Cast off 2 sts at the beginning of the next two rows (24 sts).

Next row: K1, ssK, K to last 3 sts, K2tog, K1 (22 sts).

Starting with a purl row, work 10 rows in SS.

Next row: K7, cast off 8 sts, k6 (leaving two groups of 7 sts)

Working over the first set of sts, purl 1 row.

Next row: K2tog, K5 (6 sts).

Purl 1 row.

Next row: K2tog, K4 (5 sts).

Purl 1 row.

Cast off.

With WS facing, rejoin yarn to remaining 7 sts and purl 1 row.

Next row: K5, K2tog (6 sts).

Purl 1 row.

Next row: K4, K2tog (5 sts).

Purl 1 row.

Cast off.

MATERIALS
- 35m (38yd) of 4-ply (fingering) yarn in mustard yellow

NEEDLES
- 2.75mm (UK 12, US 2) and 3mm (UK 11, US 2/3) knitting needles
- Sewing needle

TENSION (GAUGE)
- 8 sts = 2.5cm (1in) worked on 3mm (UK 11, US 2/3) knitting needles

Right Front

Using 3mm (UK 11, US 2/3) knitting needles, cast on 6 sts and purl 1 row.

Next row: K1, M1, K5 (7 sts).

Purl 1 row.

Next row: K1, M1, K6 (8 sts).

Next row: Purl to last st, M1, P1 (9 sts).

Next row: K1, M1, K8 (10 sts).

Next row: Purl to last st, M1, P1 (11 sts).

Next row: K1, M1, K10 (12 sts).

Next row: Cast off 2 sts at the beginning of the row, purl to the end of the row (10 sts).

Knit 1 row.

Next row: P1, P2tog, purl to the end of the row (9 sts).

Next row: K1, ssK, K to the end of the row (8 sts).

Purl 1 row.

Repeat last two rows four more times (4 sts).

Starting with a knit row, work 6 rows in SS.

Cast off.

Left Front

Using 3mm (UK 11, US 2/3) knitting needles, cast on 6 sts and purl 1 row.

Next row: K5, M1, K1 (7 sts).

Purl 1 row.

Next row: K6, M1, K1 (8 sts).

Next row: P1, M1, Purl to end of row (9 sts).

Next row: K8, M1, K1 (10 sts).

Next row: P1, M1, purl to end of row (11 sts).

Next row: K10, M1, K1 (12 sts).

Purl 1 row.

Next row: Cast off 2 sts at the beginning of the row, knit to the end of the row (10 sts).
Next row: P to the last 3 sts, P2tog, P1 (9 sts).
Next row: K to last 3 sts, K2tog, K1 (8 sts).
Purl 1 row.
Repeat last two rows four more times (4 sts).
Starting with a knit row, work 6 rows in SS.
Cast off.
Join shoulder seams.
Using 2.75mm (UK 12, US 2) knitting needles and with RS facing, pick up and knit as follows:
6 sts along bottom front edge, 9 sts around front shaping, 10 sts along sloped neck edge, 14 sts along shoulder, back neck and shoulder edge, 10 sts along sloped neck edge, 9 sts around front shaping and 6 sts along bottom front edge (64 sts).

Next row: (P2, K2) to end of row.
Repeat last row three more times.
Cast off.

Sleeves

With RS facing and using 3mm (UK 11, US 2/3) knitting needles, pick up and knit 30 sts around the armhole edge.
Starting with a purl row, work 7 rows in SS.
Change to 2.75mm (UK 12, US 2) knitting needles.
Next row: (K2, P2) to last 2 sts, K2.
Next row: (P2, K2) to last 2 sts, P2.
Repeat last two rows once more.
Cast off in rib.
Repeat for second sleeve.

Making up

Sew all ends of yarn in and lightly press. Sew the seam underneath one sleeve and the side seam. Repeat for the other side.

TROUSERS

MATERIALS
- 35m (38yd) of 4-ply (fingering) yarn in blue

TOOLS
- 2.75mm (UK 12, US 2) and 3mm (UK 11, US 2/3) knitting needles
- Sewing needle

SIZE
- 8 sts = 2.5cm (1in) on 3mm (UK 11, US 2/3) knitting needles

Instructions

Trouser leg (make two)

Starting at the waistband and using 3mm (UK 11, US 2/3) knitting needles, cast on 24 sts and, starting with a knit row, work 4 rows in SS.

Next row: Purl 1 row (to form a fold line).
Starting with a purl row, work 13 rows in SS.
Next row: K1, M1, K to last st, M1, K1 (26 sts).
Next row: P1, M1, P to last st, M1, P1 (28 sts).
Repeat last two rows once more (32 sts).
Starting with a knit row, continue in SS until work measures 3.5cm (1^{3}/$_{8}$in) from the last increase row, ending with a RS row.
Change to 2.75mm (UK 12, US 2) knitting needles and knit 1 row.
Cast off.

Making up

Taking one trouser leg, sew the leg seam to the start of the shaping for the gusset. Repeat for the second leg. Place the trouser legs together and sew the seam around from the front to the back at the point of the tail. Leave a gap for the tail and continue to sew the seam to the top of the trousers. Fold the top edge of the trousers over at the fold line, attaching the lower edge to the inside of the trousers.

The back of the trousers showing the hole for the tail.

FABRIC SKIRT

The skirt pattern is used for the denim skirt (page 105) and the mouse pattern skirt (page 100).

MATERIALS
- Small amount of fabric of your choice
- Sewing thread to match fabric
- Small length of 4mm elastic

TOOLS
- Sewing machine or sewing needle
- Darning needle or bodkin

SIZE
- Approx. 7cm (2¾in) from waist to hem

Instructions

1 Cut out the fabric using the template on page 142. You will need 1 x skirt piece.

2 Thread your sewing machine with matching thread and see page 11 for settings to use for stitch length and width.

3 Neaten the edges by zigzagging all the way round.

4 Fold and press top and bottom long edges with a seam allowance of 1.5cm (⅝in).

5 With RS together, pin the short ends together and stitch the side seam using a straight stitch and a seam allowance of 1cm (⅜in).

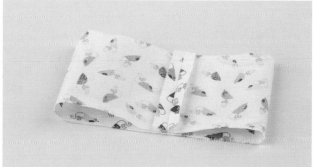

6 Press the seam open.

7 Remove the sleeve arm from the sewing machine and with WS facing, start at the back seam and sew the hem all the way round using a straight stitch.

8 Starting 1cm ($^3/_8$in) below the back seam, repeat for the other side, leaving a gap at the end, through which to thread the elastic. Leave a long thread to hand sew once the elastic has been inserted.

9 Without cutting the elastic, thread it onto a darning needle or bodkin, and push the needle into the seam. Thread the elastic through, bringing it out of the other side of the seam.

10 Tighten the elastic, gathering the fabric as you go until it fits the animal's waist, then tie a knot in the elastic. Trim the ends of the elastic then slide the knot into the seam.

11 Take the tail end of the thread that you left in step 8 to the back of the garment and hand sew the gap in the seam.

FELT DRESS

MATERIALS
- Small amounts of felt, cotton fabric and fusible interfacing
- Sewing thread to match
- Two buttons to match fabric

TOOLS
- Sewing machine or sewing needle

SIZE
- Approx. 12cm (4¾in) long from mid-neckline

Instructions

1 Using the templates on pages 139 and 142, cut out all the pieces except the heart (see step 10). You will need: 1 x felt top front, 2 x felt top backs, 1 x fabric skirt piece and a small piece of fabric for the heart later on.

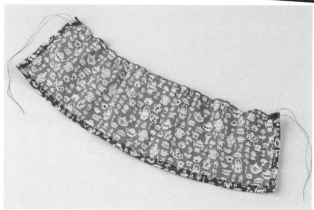

2 Machine sew a zigzag stitch around the edge of the skirt section. Press a 5mm (¼in) seam across one long edge and both short edges and sew this seam with a straight stitch; this will be the bottom of the skirt section. Using a long straight stitch, sew two lines across the top edge of the skirt approximately 3mm (⅛in) apart, then pull the thread ends gently to gather the waist edge of the skirt.

3 Pin the two back bodice pieces to the front at the shoulders and sew across the seams, as shown.

4 Press the shoulder seams open carefully, then sew a topstitch around the edge of the armholes and the bodice and neckline.

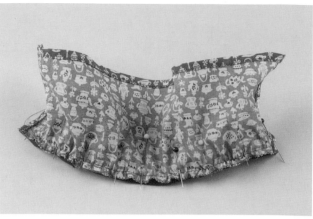

5 With RS together, sew the sides seams of the bodice using a straight stitch and press the side seams open.

6 With RS together, pin the gathered edge of the skirt to the lower edge of the bodice, ensuring that the gathers are evenly distributed. Then machine stitch the two pieces together using a straight stitch.

7 Press the seam downwards and hand sew over each end of the seam to keep it in place.

8 Sew the two buttons in place, making sure you space them evenly along the bodice back.

9 Place pins in the opposite side to line up with the buttons and make a hole for the start of the buttonhole with a seam ripper. Using a pair of small, sharp scissors, cut the buttonhole to the appropriate length to match the buttons.

10 Taking a square of fabric and a square of fusible interfacing, iron the two layers together and cut out a heart using the template on page 139. Pin it to the front of the dress. Sew in place using blanket stitch and thread in a matching colour.

103

IN THE SNOW

page 116

page 108

page 117

page 108

page 68

page 108

page 106

page 112

page 106

page 114

page 117

page 116

page 63

page 99

page 64

COAT

MATERIALS

For the Grey coat:
- 68m (74yd) of 4-ply (fingering) yarn in grey (MC)
- 14m (15yd) of 4-ply (fingering) yarn in pink (CC)

For the Brown coat:
- 68m (74yd) of 4-ply (fingering) yarn in brown (MC)
- 14m (15yd) of 4-ply (fingering) yarn in beige (CC)
- Black embroidery thread
- Three 10mm buttons

TOOLS

- 2.75mm (UK 12, US 2) and 3mm (UK 11, US 2/3) knitting needles
- Stitch markers
- Stitch holders or spare needles
- Sewing needle

TENSION (GAUGE)

- 7 sts = 2.5cm (1in) worked in GS on 3mm (UK 11, US 2/3) knitting needles

Instructions

Note:

The coat is knitted in one piece from the top down.

Using 3mm (UK 11, US 2/3) knitting needles, cast on 48 sts and knit 2 rows.

Place stitch markers as follows:

After 8th, 18th, 30th and 40th sts.

The next row forms the first buttonholes.

Next row: K1, YO, K2tog, (K to 1st before M, M1, K1, SM, K1, M1) four times, knit to last 3 sts, K2tog, YO, K1 (56 sts).

Knit 1 row.

Next row: (K to 1st before M, M1, K1, SM, K1, M1) four times, knit to end of row (64 sts).

Knit 1 row.

Repeat the last two rows five more times (104 sts).

Next row: K1, YO, K2tog, (K to 1st before M, M1, K1, SM, K1, M1) four times, knit to last 3 sts, K2tog, YO, K1 (112 sts).

Knit 1 row.

Remove markers and divide for sleeves as follows, placing the stitches on holders:

K16 front sts, K26 sleeve sts, K28 back sts, K26 sleeve sts, K16 front sts.

Starting with one set of 26 sleeve sts and with WS facing, cast on 2 sts at the beginning of the next two rows (30 sts).

Continue in GS (knit every row) until sleeve measures 2cm (¾in), ending with a WS row.

Change to CC yarn and 2.75mm (UK 12, US 2) knitting needles and knit 2 rows.

Cast off.

Repeat for second sleeve.

Continuing with the fronts and back of the coat and using 3mm (UK 11, US 2/3) knitting needles, start with a WS row and work across the body of the coat as follows:

Next row: K16 front sts, cast on 4 sts, K26 back sts, cast on 4 sts, K16 front sts. (66 sts).

Knit 10 rows.

Next row: K1, YO, K2tog, Knit to last 3 sts, K2tog, YO, K1.

Knit 5 rows.

Change to CC and 2.75mm (UK 12, US 2) knitting needles and knit 2 rows.

Cast off.

Front bands

With RS facing and using 2.75mm (UK 12, US 2) knitting needles and CC yarn, pick up and knit 21 sts along the front edge of the coat.

Knit 1 row.

Cast off.

Repeat for other front.

Collar

With RS facing and using 2.75mm (UK 12, US 2) knitting needles and CC yarn, pick up and knit 44 sts around neck of coat.

Next row: K1, M1, K to last st, M1, K1 (46 sts).

Next row: Knit 1 row.

Repeat last two rows twice more (50 sts).
Next row: K1, ssK, K to last 3 sts, K2togtbl, K1 (48 sts).
Repeat last row once more (46 sts).
Cast off.

Pocket (make two)

Using CC and 2.75mm (UK 12, US 2) knitting needles, cast on 8 sts and work as follows:
Next row: K3, turn work.
Next row: P3, turn work.
Repeat the last two rows twice more.
Next row: K across all sts.
Next row: P3, turn work.
Next row: K3, turn work.
Repeat last two rows twice more.
Next row: Purl across all sts.
Next row: K1, M1, K to last st, M1, K1 (10 sts).
Starting with a purl row, work 5 rows in SS.
Next row: ssK, K to last 2 sts, K2tog (8 sts).
Next row: P2tog, P4, P2togtbl (6 sts).
Next row: ssK, K2, K2togtbl (4 sts).
Cast off (WS).

Making up

Sew the seams on the sleeves, matching colours. Lightly press, sew in ends of yarn and sew the buttons to the buttonband using matching yarn.

Taking a pocket and black embroidery thread, embroider two small stitches for eyes and a French knot for the nose. Catch the cast-on edge of each ear on the pocket to the inside edge. Repeat for the second pocket. Pin in place on the fronts of the coat and sew around the sides and bottom with matching yarn, leaving the top open.

Top Tip!

If you work the buttonholes at both ends of the row it is easy to place the buttons – just sew them over the buttonhole.

SWEATER

MATERIALS

For the Frog Sweater:

- 55m (60yd) of 4-ply (fingering) yarn in navy blue (MC)
- Small amounts of 4-ply (fingering) yarn in orange, white and black

For the Robin Sweater:

- 55m (60yd) of 4-ply (fingering) yarn in pale blue (MC)
- Small amounts of 4-ply (fingering) yarn in white, red, dark brown and black

For the Mouse Sweater:

- 55m (60yd) of 4-ply (fingering) yarn in turquoise (MC)
- Small amounts of 4-ply (fingering) yarn in pink, grey and black

TOOLS

- 2.75mm (UK 12, US 2) and 3mm (UK 11, US 2/3) knitting needles
- Sewing needle

TENSION (GAUGE)

- 8 sts = 2.5cm (1in) on 3mm (UK 11, US 2/3) knitting needles

Instructions

Front

Using 2.75mm (UK 12, US 2) knitting needles and MC, cast on 32 sts and work as follows:

Next row: (K2, P2) repeat to end of row.

Repeat the last row three more times to work the rib.

Change to 3mm (UK 11, US 2/3) knitting needles and, starting with a knit row, work 14 rows in SS.

At the same time, follow your chosen chart motif (see page 111), joining in colours as necessary.

Cast off 2 sts at the beginning of the next two rows (28 sts).

Next row: K1, ssK, K to last 3 sts, K2tog, K1 (26 sts)*.

Starting with a purl row, work 5 rows in SS.

Next row: K9, cast off 8 sts, K8 (leaving two groups of 9 sts).

Working over the first set of sts, purl 1 row.

Next row: K1, ssK, K6 (8 sts).
Purl 1 row.

Next row: K1, ssK, K5 (7 sts).
Purl 1 row.

Next row: K1, ssK, K4 (6 sts).
Purl 1 row.

Next row: K1, ssK, K3 (5 sts).
Purl 1 row.
Cast off.

With WS facing, rejoin yarn to remaining 9 sts and purl 1 row.

Next row: K6, K2tog, K1 (8 sts).
Purl 1 row.

Next row: K5, K2tog, K1 (7 sts).
Purl 1 row.

Next row: K4, K2tog, K1 (6 sts).
Purl 1 row.

Next row: K3, K2tog, K1 (5 sts).
Purl 1 row.
Cast off.

Back

Work as for Front to * (omitting the motif).

Starting with a purl row, work 11 rows in SS.

Next row: K8, cast off 10 sts, K7 (leaving two groups of 8 sts).

Working over the first set of sts, purl 1 row.

Next row: Cast off 3 sts, K to end of row (5 sts).

Purl 1 row.

Cast off.

With RS facing, rejoin yarn to remaining 8 sts and knit 1 row.

Next row: Cast off 3 sts, P to end of row (5 sts).

Knit 1 row.

Cast off.

Neckband

Join right shoulder seam.

Using 2.75mm (UK 12, US 2) knitting needles and MC with RS facing, pick up and knit 22 sts along the front neck edge and 18 sts along the back neck edge (40 sts).

Work 4 rows in K2, P2 rib.

Cast off.

Sleeves

Join left shoulder seam and start with one armhole.

With RS facing and using 3mm (UK 11, US 2/3) knitting needles and MC, pick up and knit 30 sts around the armhole edge.

Starting with a purl row, work 7 rows in SS.

Change to 2.75mm (UK 12, US 2) knitting needles and work 4 rows in K2, P2 rib.

Cast off.

Repeat for second sleeve.

Making up

Using the photographs for guidance, work the embroidery shown for your design using your chosen colours. Sew the sleeve and side seams.

Frog chart

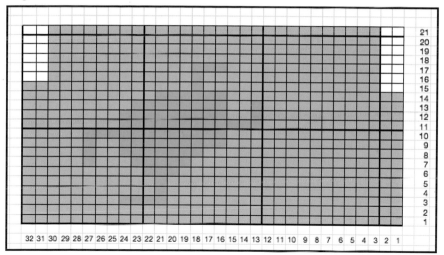

Robin chart

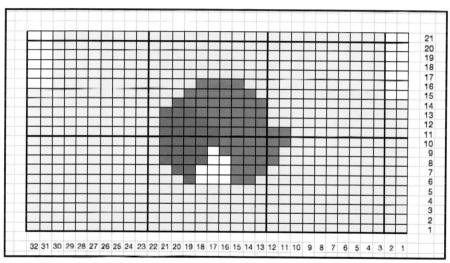

Mouse chart

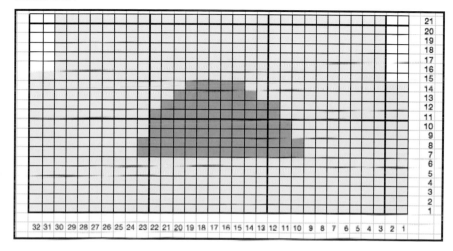

LACE TOP

Instructions

Front

Using MC and 3.25mm (UK 10, US 3) knitting needles, cast on 36 sts and knit 2 rows.

Change to CC yarn and work as follows:

Next row: ((K2tog) twice, (K1, YO) four times, (K2tog) twice), three times.

Purl 1 row.

Repeat last 2 rows twice more.

Change to 3mm (UK 11, US 2/3) knitting needles and MC yarn, and knit 3 rows.

Purl 1 row.

Next row: K1, ssK, K to last 3 sts, K2tog, K1 (34 sts).

Purl 1 row.

Repeat last 2 rows three more times (28 sts).

Cast off 2 sts at the beginning of the next 2 rows (24 sts).

Next row: K1, ssK, K to last 3 sts, K2tog, K1 (22 sts).

Purl 1 row*.

Shape neck as follows:

Next row: K7, cast off 8, K6 (leaving two groups of 7 sts).

Turn, and working over first set of 7 sts only, purl 1 row.

Next row: K1, ssK, K4 (6 sts).

MATERIALS

- 30m (33yd) of 4-ply (fingering) yarn in cherry red (MC)
- 6m (7yd) of 4-ply (fingering) yarn in fuchsia pink (CC)

TOOLS

- 2.75mm (UK 12, US 2), 3mm (UK 11, US 2/3) and 3.25mm (UK 10, US 3) knitting needles
- Sewing needle

TENSION (GAUGE)

- 8 sts = 2.5cm (1in) on 3mm (UK 11, US 2/3) knitting needles

Purl 1 row.

Next row: K1, ssK, K3 (5 sts).

Purl 1 row.

Next row: K1, ssK, K2 (4 sts).

Starting with a purl row, work 3 rows in SS.

Cast off.

With WS facing, rejoin yarn to remaining 7 sts and purl 1 row.

Next row: K4, K2tog, K1 (6 sts).

Purl 1 row.

Next row: K3, K2tog, K1 (5 sts).

Purl 1 row.

Next row, K2, K2tog, K1 (4 sts).

Continuing in SS, work 3 rows.

Cast off.

Back

Work as for Front to *.

Continuing in SS, work 4 rows.

Next row: K5, cast off 12, K4 (leaving two groups of 5 sts).

Purl 1 row.

Next row: K1, ssK, K2 (4 sts).

Starting with a purl row, work 3 rows in SS.

Cast off.

With WS facing rejoin yarn to remaining 5 sts and purl 1 row.

Next row: K2, K2tog, K1 (4 sts).

Starting with a purl row, work 3 rows in SS.

Cast off.

Neck edge

Join right shoulder seam.

Using 2.75mm (UK 12, US 2) knitting needles and CC yarn, pick up and knit 21 sts along the front neck edge and 18 sts along the back neck edge (39 sts).

Knit 1 row.

Cast off using a picot cast-off as follows:

Cast off 2 sts, *sl st back to LH needle, cast on 2 sts, cast off 4 sts*.

Repeat from * to * to last st, cast off remaining st.

Armhole edge

Join left shoulder seam and starting with one armhole.

Using 2.75mm (UK 12, US 2) knitting needles and CC yarn, pick up and knit 26 sts around the armhole edge.

Knit 1 row.

Cast off using a picot cast-off as follows:

Cast off 2 sts, (*sl st back to LH needle, cast on 2 sts, cast off 4 sts*.)

Repeat from * to * to end of row.

Repeat for second armhole.

Making up

Sew in all loose ends of yarn and sew the side seams using matching yarn colours.

Press lightly with a steam iron.

TIGHTS

Instructions

Note:

Each heel is knitted using short row shaping. You start by working one less stitch on each row to create the heel shape. Once you have reached the middle of the heel you work outwards again, working one extra stitch on every row to get back to the top of the heel. By picking up a 'loop' before the extra stitch you ensure there are no gaps in the heel. The heel and toe are worked over half the row (11 sts).

There are right and left legs; the seam will be on the inside of the leg.

Right leg

Using MC yarn and 2.75mm (UK 12, US 2) needles, cast on 26 sts and work rib as follows:
Next row: (K2, P2), K2.
Next row: (P2, K2), P2.
Repeat last 2 rows once more.
Change to 3mm (UK 11, US 2/3) knitting needles.
Starting with a knit row, work 8 rows in SS.
Next row: K10, ssK, K2, K2tog, K10 (24 sts).
Starting with a purl row, work 3 rows in SS.
Next row: K9, ssK, K2, K2tog, K9 (22 sts).
Starting with a purl row, work 5 rows in SS.

Front of the tights.

Back of the tights showing the hole for the tail.

MATERIALS

- 30m (33yd) of 4-ply (fingering) yarn in cherry red (MC)
- 10m (11yd) of 4-ply (fingering) yarn in fuchsia pink (CC)

TOOLS

- Two 2 .75mm (UK 12, US 2) and three 3mm (UK 11, US 2/3) knitting needles
- Four stitch markers
- Sewing needle

TENSION (GAUGE)

- 8 sts = 2.5cm (1in) on 3mm (UK 11, US 2/3) knitting needles

Place marker at each end of the row to mark the start of the leg.
Starting with a knit row, work 2 rows in SS.
Change to CC and work 2 rows in SS.
Change to MC and work 2 rows in SS.
Change to CC and work 2 rows in SS.
Repeat last 4 rows twice more. Change to MC and work 2 rows in SS.
Using CC knit 1 row**.
Break yarn and slide sts to LH needle and, with RS facing, start the heel shaping by knitting 11 sts in CC.
Turn work and work as follows:
Note: All sts are slipped purlwise.
Next row: sl1, P10, turn.
Next row: sl1, K9, turn.
Next row: sl1, P8, turn.
Next row: sl1, K7, turn.
Next row: sl1, P6, turn.
Next row: sl1, K5, turn.
You will now start working outwards again, working one extra stitch on each row.
Next row: sl1, P4, pick up bar before the next stitch and purl together with the stitch, turn.
Next row: sl1, K5, pick up bar before the next stitch and knit together with the stitch, turn.
Next row: sl1, P6, pick up bar before the next stitch and purl together with the stitch, turn.
Next row: sl1, K7, pick up bar before the next stitch and knit together with the stitch, turn.
Next row: sl1, P8, pick up bar before the next stitch and purl together with the stitch, turn.
Next row: sl1, K9, pick up bar before the next stitch and knit together with the stitch, knit to the end of the row.

Break CC yarn, slide sts to LH needle and rejoin MC. With RS facing and starting with a knit row, work 2 rows in SS.
Change to CC and work 2 rows in SS.
Change to MC and work 2 rows in SS.
Change to CC and work toe shaping as follows:
Next row: K1, ssK, K5, K2tog, K2, ssK, K5, K2tog, K1 (18 sts).
Purl 1 row.
Next row: K1, ssK, K3, K2tog, K2, ssK, K3, K2tog, K1 (14 sts).
Next row: P1, P2tog, P1, P2togtbl, P2, P2tog, P1, P2togtbl, P1 (10 sts).
Cast off using three-needle cast-off technique (see page 18)

Left leg

Work as for right leg to **.
Start the heel shaping with WS facing by purling 11 sts in CC.

Turn work and work as follows using CC yarn:
Note: All sts are slipped purlwise.
Next row: sl1, K10, turn.
Next row: sl1, P9, turn.
Next row: sl1, K8, turn.
Next row: sl1, P7, turn.
Next row: sl1, K6, turn.
Next row: sl1, P5, turn.
You will now start working outwards again, working one extra stitch on each row.
Next row: sl1, K4, pick up bar before the next stitch and knit together with the stitch, turn.
Next row: sl1, P5, pick up bar before the next stitch and purl together with the stitch, turn.
Next row: sl1, K6, pick up bar before the next stitch and knit together with the stitch, turn.
Next row: sl1, P7, pick up bar before the next stitch and purl together with the stitch, turn.
Next row: sl1, K8, pick up bar before the next stitch and knit together with the stitch, turn.
Next row: sl1, P9, pick up bar before the next stitch and purl together with the stitch, purl to end of row.
Change to MC and work 2 rows in SS.
Change to CC and work 2 rows in SS.
Change to MC and work 2 rows in SS.
Change to CC and work toe shaping as follows:
Next row: K1, ssK, K5, K2tog, K2, ssK, K5, K2tog, K1 (18 sts).
Purl 1 row.
Next row: K1, ssK, K3, K2tog, K2, ssK, K3, K2tog, K1 (14 sts).
Next row: P1, P2tog, P1, P2togtbl, P2, P2tog, P1, P2togtbl, P1 (10 sts).
Cast off using the three-needle cast-off technique (see page 18).

Making up

Taking one leg, sew the side seam from the toe up to the stitch marker, which marks the top of the leg. Repeat for the second leg.

Starting at the top of the tights, sew the two legs together, leaving a gap of approximately 1cm (³/₈in) in the back seam for the tail.

MITTENS

MATERIALS
- 17m (19yd) of 4-ply (fingering) yarn in pink or pale brown

TOOLS
- 2.75mm (UK 12, US 2) knitting needles and 3mm (UK 11, US 2/3) DPN
- Sewing needle

TENSION (GAUGE)
- 8 sts = 2.5cm (1in) worked in SS on 3mm (UK 11, US 2/3) knitting needles

Instructions

Mitten (make two)

Using 2.75mm (UK 12, US 2) knitting needles, cast on 24 sts and work as follows:

Next row: (K2, P2) to end of row.

Repeat last row three more times to form rib of mitten.

Change to 3mm (UK 11, US 2/3) knitting needles and, starting with a knit row, work 6 rows in st st.

Next row: K1, ssK, K7, K2tog, ssK, K7, K2tog, K1 (20 sts).

Purl 1 row.

Next row: K1, ssK, K5, K2tog, ssK, K5, K2tog, K1 (16 sts).

Purl 1 row.

Next row: K1, ssK, K3, K2tog, ssK, K3, K2tog, K1 (12 sts).

Next row: P1, P2tog, P1, P2togtbl, P2tog, P1, P2togtbl, P1 (8 sts).

Thread yarn through remaining sts, leaving a long enough tail for making up.

Cord

Using 3mm (UK 11, US 2/3) DPN, cast on 2 sts and work an i-cord (see page 33 under *Ear edging*) until work measures 19cm (7½in).

Making up

Gather the cast-off end of the mitten and sew the side seam. Repeat for second mitten. Sew one end of the cord inside the mitten at the bottom of the rib section, making sure the stitches do not show on the RS. Sew the second mitten to the other end of the cord in the same way.

HATS

MATERIALS

- 24m (26yd) of 4-ply (fingering) yarn in pink or pale brown

TOOLS

- 2.75mm (UK 12, US 2) and 3mm (UK 11, US 2/3) knitting needles
- Three stitch markers
- 20mm (¾in) pompom maker
- Sewing needle

TENSION (GAUGE)

- 8 sts = 2.5cm (1in) on 3mm (UK 11, US 2/3) knitting needles worked in SS

Instructions

Beanie hat

Using 2.75mm (UK 12, US 2) knitting needles and chosen yarn colour, cast on 48 sts and work as follows:
Next row: (K2, P2) to end of row.
Repeat this row nine more times to work rib section.
Change to 3mm (UK 11, US 2/3) knitting needles and, starting with a knit row, work 14 rows in SS.
Prepare for shaping the crown.
Place a marker after the 12th, 24th and 36th sts.
Next row: K1, ssK, (K to 2 sts before M, K2tog, SM, ssK) three times, K to last 3 sts, K2tog, K1 (40 sts).
Purl 1 row.
Repeat last 2 rows three more times (16 sts).
Next row: (K2tog) eight times (8 sts).
Thread yarn through sts, leaving a long enough length for sewing up.

Making up

Gather the cast-off end and secure the yarn. Sew the side seam. Make a pompom using a pompom maker (or use the tip, right). Trim pompom into a neat ball and secure to the top of the hat.

Square hat

Using 2.75mm (UK 12, US 2) knitting needles and chosen yarn colour, cast on 48 sts and work as follows:
Next row: (K2, P2) to end of row.
Repeat this row nine more times to work rib section.
Change to 3mm (UK 11, US 2/3) knitting needles and, starting with a knit row, work 24 rows in SS.
Cast off.

Making up

Sew the side seam. Note that the purl side of the work is the RS. With the side seam in the middle of the work, sew the seam across the top of the hat. Make two pompoms using a pompom maker (or use the tip below). Trim pompoms into neat balls and secure to the top of the hat.

Top Tip!

You can make tiny pompoms using a fork. Wrap the yarn around around the prongs until it looks thick enough and tie a piece of yarn tightly through the middle of the prongs, around your wraps to secure it. Slide the pompom off the fork and trim. Dangle the pompom over a boiling kettle (tied onto a wooden spoon to avoid scalding yourself!) and the steam will 'fluff' up the pompom!

AND SO TO BED

page 126

page 122-3

page 122-3

page 65

page 124-5

page 120

page 68

page 121

page 130

page 127

page 65

page 131

page 131

page 68

DRESSING GOWN

Top Tip!
When working in moss stitch (MS), place a marker on the RS of the work as a reminder. You will need to know so that when you work the collar pieces they are in the right place.

Instructions

Note:
This is worked in MS throughout. To work MS over an even number of sts:
Row 1: K1, P1 to end of row.
Row 2: P1, K1 to end of row.
Therefore you work a purl stitch over a knit stitch and a knit stitch over a purl stitch.

Back
Cast on 36 sts and work in MS until work measures 3cm (1¼in).
Next row: K2tog, work to last 2 sts, K2tog (34 sts).
Continue in MS and repeat this decrease row when work measures 5cm (2in), 7cm (2¾in) and 8cm (3¹/₈in) (28 sts).
Continue in MS and when work measures 9cm (3½in), cast off 2 sts at the beginning of the next 2 rows (24 sts).
Next row: K2tog, work to last 2 sts, K2tog (22 sts).
Repeat last row once more (20 sts).
Continue in MS until armhole measures 5cm (2in).
Cast off.

Front (make two)
Cast on 18 sts and work in MS until work measures 3cm (1¼in).
Next row: K2tog, K to end of row (17 sts).
Continue in MS and repeat this decrease row when work measures 5cm (2in), 7cm (2¾in) and 8cm (3¹/₈in) (14 sts).
Continue in MS and when work measures 9cm (3½in), work as follows:
Next row: Cast off 2 sts at the beginning of the row, K to last st, M1, K1 (13 sts).
Next row: Work to last 2 sts, K2tog (12 sts).
Next row: K2tog, work to end of row (11 sts).
Continue in MS until armhole measures 5cm (2in), ending at armhole edge.

Next row: Cast off 5 sts, K to end of row.
Working over the remaining 6 sts, work 7 rows in MS to form the collar.
Cast off.

Sleeve (make two)

Pin the back to the fronts with RS on the outside and join the shoulder seams. (The two collar pieces will be at the neck edge.)
To make the sleeves, with RS facing, pick up and knit 26 sts around the armhole edge.
Work 18 rows in MS.
Cast off.
Repeat for second sleeve.

Pocket (make two)

Cast on 10 sts and work 16 rows in MS.
Cast off.

Belt

Cast on 72 sts and knit 2 rows.
Cast off.

Belt loop (make two)

Cast on 5 sts and knit 1 row.
Cast off.

Making up

Sew the side seams under the sleeve and down each side of the dressing gown. Pin the belt loops in place on each side seam, using the photograph for guidance, and sew them in place.

Embroider a flower on one pocket using embroidery thread and lazy daisy stitches (see page 23). Pin the pocket in place on the right front of the dressing gown, and the second pocket in place on the left front and sew them on. Sew each end of the collar together at the neck and ease to fit the back neck, then sew in place.

SLIPPERS

MATERIALS
- 20m (22yd) of 4-ply (fingering) yarn in pink
- Embroidery thread in pink, yellow and green

TOOLS
- 2.75mm (UK 12, US 2) and 3mm (UK 11, US 2/3) knitting needles
- Sewing needle

TENSION
- 8 sts = 2.5cm (1in) in SS on 3mm (UK 11, US 2/3) knitting needles

Instructions

Slipper (make two)

Cast on 4 sts using 3mm (UK 11, US 2/3) needles and knit 1 row.
Next row: K1, M1, K to last st, M1, K1 (6 sts).
Knit 1 row.
Repeat the last 2 rows three more times (12 sts).
Knit 6 rows.
Next row: K1, K2tog, K to last 3 sts, K2tog, K1 (10 sts).
Knit 1 row.
Repeat the last two rows twice more (6 sts).
Next row: K1, (K2tog) twice, K1 (4 sts).
Cast on 14 sts at the beginning of the next two rows (32 sts).
Continue in SS.
Starting with a knit row, work 2 rows in SS.
Next row: K12, ssK, K4, K2tog, K12 (30 sts).
Next row: P12, P2tog, P2, P2togtbl, P12 (28 sts).
Next row: K11, ssK, K2, K2tog, K11 (26 sts).
Next row: P10, P2tog, P2, P2togtbl, P10 (24 sts).
Change to 2.75mm (UK 12, US 2) knitting needles and knit 3 rows.
Cast off.

Making up

Sew the seam joining the back of the slipper. Fold the sole up and sew to the lower edge of the side of the slipper. Repeat for the second slipper. With embroidery thread, embroider a flower and leaves on the front of each slipper using lazy daisy stitch (see page 23).

PANTS, VEST & SOCKS

Instructions

> **Note:**
> The pants are made in one piece, starting at the front.

Pants

Using MC and 3mm (UK 11, US 2/3) knitting needles, cast on 4 sts and, starting with a knit row, work 4 rows in SS.
Next row: K1, M1, K to last st, M1, K1 (6 sts).
Next row: P1, M1, P to last st, M1, P1 (8 sts).
Next row: K1, M1, K to last st, M1, K1 (10 sts).
Purl 1 row.
Cast on 3 sts at the beginning of the next 2 rows (16 sts).
Cast on 2 sts at the beginning of the next 2 rows (20 sts).
Starting with a knit row, work 2 rows in SS.
Next row: K1, M1, K to last st, M1, K1 (22 sts).
Starting with a purl row, work 3 rows in SS.
Change to 2.75mm (UK 12, US 2) knitting needles and CC and knit 3 rows.
Cast off.
With RS facing and using 3mm (UK 11, US 2/3) knitting needles and MC, pick up and knit 4 sts from cast-on edge of knitted piece.
Next row: P1, M1, P to last st, M1, P1 (6 sts).
Cast on 2 sts at the beginning of the next 6 rows (18 sts).
Next row: K1, M1, K6, cast off 4 sts, K5, M1, K1 (making two groups of 8 sts).
Next row: P8, (M1) four times, P8 (20 sts).
The last 2 rows form a hole for the tail to thread through.
Next row: K1, M1, K to last st, M1, K1 (22 sts).
Starting with a purl row, work 5 rows in SS.
Change to 2.75mm (UK 12, US 2) knitting needles and CC and knit 3 rows.
Cast off.

MATERIALS: PANTS
- 15m (16yd) of 4-ply (fingering) yarn in pink or cream (MC)
- 4m (4yd) of 4-ply (fingering) yarn in cream or pink (CC)

TOOLS
- 2.75mm (UK 12, US 2) and 3mm (UK 11, US 2/3) knitting needles
- Sewing needle

TENSION (GAUGE)
- 8 sts = 2.5cm (1in) in SS on 3mm (UK 11, US 2/3) knitting needles

Leg edging

Using CC and 3mm (UK 11, US 2/3) knitting needles, pick up and knit 12 sts along the sloped leg edge to the centre bottom seam. Pick up and knit a further 12 sts along the second half of the leg edge (24 sts).
Knit 1 row.
Cast off.
Repeat for second leg edge.

Making up

Sew the side seams of the pants, matching colours as you sew. For the boy's pants, embroider the 'Y' front using chain stitch (see page 22) and CC.

Vest

Front

Using CC and 2.75mm (UK 12, US 2) knitting needles, cast on 24 sts and knit 3 rows.

Change to 3mm (UK 11, US 2/3) knitting needles and MC, and, starting with a knit row, work 10 rows in SS.

Cast off 2 sts at the beginning of the next 2 rows (20 sts).

Next row: K1, ssK, K to last 3 sts, K2tog, K1 (18 sts).

Purl 1 row**.

Next row: K7, cast off 4 sts, K6 (leaving 2 groups of 7 sts).

Turn work and working over first set of 7 sts only work as follows:

Purl 1 row.

Next row: K1, ssK, K4 (6 sts).

Next row: P3, P2togtbl, P1 (5 sts).

Next row: K1, ssK, K2 (4 sts).

Starting with a purl row, work 5 rows in SS.

Cast off.

With WS facing, rejoin MC to remaining 7 sts and work as follows:

Purl 1 row.

Next row: K4, K2tog, K1 (6 sts).

Next row: P1, P2tog, P3 (5 sts).

MATERIALS: VEST

- 18m (20yd) of 4-ply (fingering) yarn in pink or cream (MC)
- 6m (7yd) of 4-ply (fingering) yarn in cream or blue (CC)

TOOLS

- 2.75mm (UK 12, US 2) and 3mm (UK 11, US 2/3) knitting needles
- Sewing needle

TENSION (GAUGE)

- 8 sts = 2.5cm (1in) in SS on 3mm (UK 11, US 2/3) knitting needles

Next row: K2, K2tog, K1 (4 sts).

Starting with a purl row, work 5 rows in SS.

Cast off.

Back

Work from beginning of pattern for front to **.

Starting with a knit row, work a further 4 rows in SS.

Next row: K6, cast off 6 sts, K5 (leaving 2 groups of 6 sts).

Turn work and working over first set of 6 sts only, work as follows:

Purl 1 row.

Next row: K1, ssK, K3 (5 sts).

Next row: P2, P2togtbl, P1 (4 sts).

Starting with a knit row, work 2 rows in SS.

Cast off.

With WS facing, rejoin MC to remaining 6 sts and work as follows:

Purl 1 row.

Next row: K3, K2tog, K1 (5 sts).

Next row: P1, P2tog, P2 (4 sts).

Starting with a knit row, work 2 rows in SS.

Cast off.

Neck and armhole edging

Lightly press the front and back pieces and join the right shoulder seam.

Using CC and 2.75mm (UK 12, US 2) knitting needles, pick up and knit 20 sts around front neck shaping and 18 sts along back neck shaping (38 sts).

Knit 1 row.

Cast off.

Join left shoulder seam. Using 2.75mm (UK 12, US 2) knitting needles and CC, pick up and knit 13 sts up to the shoulder join and a further 13 sts to the bottom of the armhole (26 sts).

Knit 1 row.

Cast off.

Repeat for second armhole.

Join the side seams, matching colours.

MATERIALS: SOCKS
- 8m (9yd) of 4-ply (fingering) yarn in pink or cream (MC)
- 8m (9yd) of 4-ply (fingering) yarn in cream or blue (CC)

TOOLS
- 3mm (UK 11, US 2/3) knitting needles and a spare needle for three-needle cast-off
- Sewing needle

TENSION (GAUGE)
- 8 sts = 2.5cm (1in) in SS on 3mm (UK 11, US 2/3) knitting needles

Socks

Note:
The heel of the sock is knitted using short row shaping. You start by working one less st on each row to create the heel shape. Once you have reached the middle of the heel you work outwards again, working one extra stitch on every row to get back to the top of the heel. By picking up a 'loop' before the extra stitch, you ensure there are no gaps in the heel. The heel and toe are worked over half the row (11 sts).

There are right and left socks; the seam is on the inside of the leg.

Right sock

Using CC, cast on 22 sts and work rib as follows:

Next row: (K1, P1) 11 times.

Repeat last row twice more.

Change to MC and, starting with a knit row, work 4 rows in SS*.

With RS facing, join in and work with CC, (without breaking off MC yarn), starting the heel shaping by knitting 11 sts. Turn work and work as follows.

Note: All stitches are slipped purlwise.

Next row: sl1, P10, turn.
Next row: sl1, K9, turn.
Next row: sl1, P8, turn.
Next row: sl1, K7, turn.
Next row: sl1, P6, turn.
Next row: sl1, K5, turn.

You will now start working outwards again, working one extra stitch on each row.

Next row: sl1, P4, pick up bar before the next stitch and purl together with the stitch, turn.
Next row: sl1, K5, pick up bar before the next stitch and knit together with the stitch, turn.
Next row: sl1, P6, pick up bar before the next stitch and purl together with the stitch, turn.
Next row: sl1, K7, pick up bar before the next stitch and knit together with the stitch, turn.
Next row: sl1, P8, pick up bar before the next stitch and purl together with the stitch, turn.
Next row: sl1, K9, pick up bar before the next stitch and knit together with the stitch, wrap next stitch (which is MC) and turn (see page 14).
Next row: sl1, purl to end of row.

Change to MC and, starting with a knit row, work 5 rows in SS.

Break off MC, change to CC and purl 1 row.

Next row: K1, ssK, K5, K2tog, K2, ssK, K5, K2tog, K1 (18 sts).

Purl 1 row.

Next row: K1, ssK, K3, K2tog, K2, ssK, K3, K2tog, K1 (14 sts).

Next row: P1, P2tog, P1, P2togtbl, P2, P2tog, P1, P2togtbl, P1 (10 sts).

Cast off using three-needle cast-off technique (see page 18).

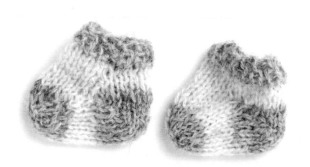

Left sock

Work as for right sock to *.

Next row: slip sts onto LH needle, break off MC and join in CC and, with WS facing, work as follows:

Work with CC, starting the heel shaping by purling 11 sts.

Turn work and work as follows:

Note: All stitches are slipped purlwise.

Next row: sl1, K10, turn.
Next row: sl1, P9, turn.
Next row: sl1, K8, turn.
Next row: sl1, P7, turn.
Next row: sl1, K6, turn.
Next row: sl1, P5, turn.

You will now start working outwards again, working one extra stitch on each row.

Next row: sl1, K4, pick up bar before the next stitch and knit together with the stitch, turn.
Next row: sl1, P5, pick up bar before the next stitch and purl together with the stitch, turn.
Next row: sl1, K6, pick up bar before the next stitch and knit together with the stitch, turn.
Next row: sl1, P7, pick up bar before the next stitch and purl together with the stitch, turn.
Next row: sl1, K8, pick up bar before the next stitch and knit together with the stitch, turn.
Next row: sl1, P9, pick up bar before the next stitch and purl together with the stitch, wrap next stitch (which is MC) and turn.
Next row: sl1, knit to end of row.

Change to MC and, starting with a purl row, work 5 rows in SS.

Change to CC, breaking off MC, and knit 1 row.

Next row: P1, P2tog, P5, P2togtbl, P2, P2tog, P5, P2togtbl, P1 (18 sts)

Knit 1 row.

Next row: P1, P2tog, P3, P2togtbl, P2, P2tog, P3, P2togtbl, P1 (14 sts).

Next row: K1, ssK, K1, K2tog, K2, ssK, K1, K2tog, K1 (10 sts).

Cast off using the three-needle cast-off technique (see page 18)

Making up

Matching the yarn colour, sew the side seam of the sock. The seam will be on the inside edge of each sock.

QUILT

MATERIALS
- Small amounts of 4-ply (fingering) yarn in six different colours
- Piece of velvet at least 4cm (1½in) larger than finished knitting
- 1m (1yd) of cotton lace
- Sewing thread to match yarn

TOOLS
- 4mm (UK 8, US 6) knitting needles
- Sewing needle

SIZE
- 26 x 23cm (10¼ x 9in)

Instructions

Knitted strip (make three)

Using a double strand of yarn, cast on 17 sts and, starting with a knit row, work 16 rows in SS. Change colour and work a further 16 rows. Repeat this colour change twice more, making a strip of 4 colours.

Make two more strips, alternating the colours.

Making up

Lightly press all three strips of knitting to stop the edges curling. Place two strips side by side and sew together. Repeat for the third strip.

Place the knitted section on top of the WS of the velvet fabric. This will also hide any untidy stitches underneath. Starting along one side, fold each edge of the fabric over twice and pin to the knitting. Repeat on remaining three sides. Trim and fold the fabric on the corners to make them neat. Using matching sewing thread and a sewing needle, sew the velvet folded edge to the knitting.

Using sewing thread to match the cotton lace, sew the lace to the velvet using the photograph for guidance.

COAT HANGER

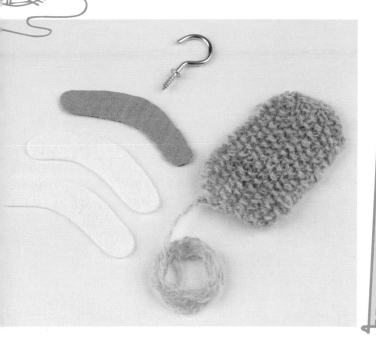

MATERIALS
- 10m (11yd) of 4-ply (fingering) yarn in blue, pink or cream
- Thick cardboard with a corrugated centre
- Small piece of white felt
- Cup hook 2.5cm (1in) in length
- Glue
- Small amount of cream ribbon
- Sewing thread to match ribbon

TOOLS
- 3mm (UK 11, US 2/3) knitting needles
- Sewing needle

SIZE
- 8cm (3¹⁄₈in) long

Instructions

Cast on 8 sts and work 2 rows in MS (see page 120).
Next row: Kfb, work in MS to last st, Kfb (10 sts).
Continue in MS until work measures 5cm (2in).
Next row: K2tog, work in MS to last 2 sts, K2tog (8 sts).
Work 2 rows in MS.

Cast off, leaving a long tail end.
Next, cut out the cardboard and white felt pieces (as shown above) using the template on page 139, and follow the steps below to make up the coat hanger.

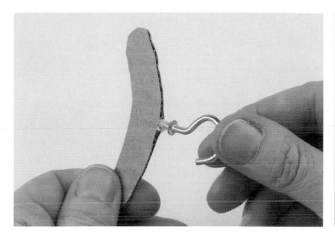

1 Place some glue on the cuphook and screw it into the top centre of the cardboard template.

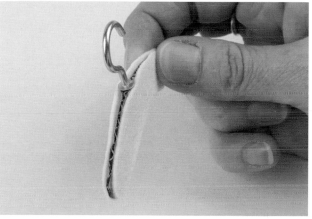

2 Glue the felt pieces to either side of the cardboard and allow to dry.

3 Fold the knitted piece lengthwise with RS together and thread over the cuphook.

4 Pull the knitted piece down over the stiff felt and cardboard section.

5 With the long tail end of the yarn, sew the seam over the felt template and secure the yarn end.

6 The knitted section now covers the felt template completely.

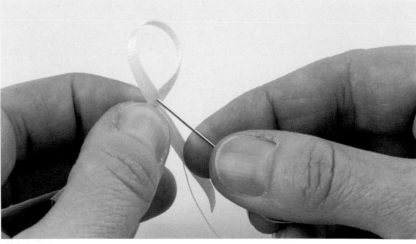

7 Loop the length of cream ribbon and secure with a stitch.

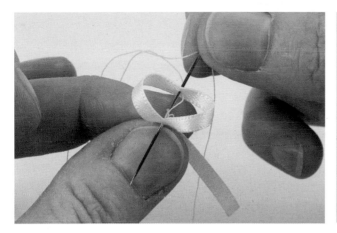

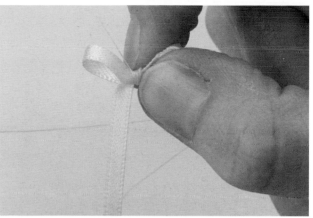

8 Bring the needle through from the back to the front of the ribbon to form a bow.

9 Pull tight and wrap the thread around the centre. Secure with a stitch to form a bow.

11 Trim the ends of the ribbon to length diagonally so they do not fray.

10 Attach the bow to the front of the coat hanger with the sewing thread.

The finished coat hanger.

MATTRESS, SHEET & PILLOW

Instructions

Mattress

1 Fold the fabric in half with RS together so that the folded piece measures 17 x 28cm (6¾ x 11in).

2 Using a straight stitch on your sewing machine, sew along one short edge and the long edge leaving a 1cm (³/₈in) seam allowance. Turn through and press the seams.

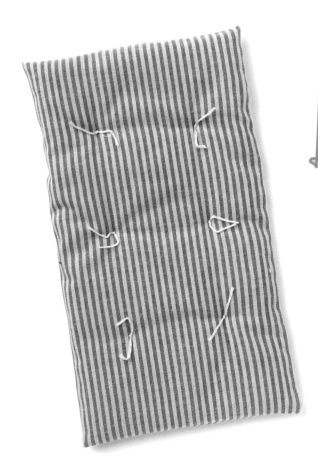

MATERIALS AND TOOLS

For the Mattress:
- Fabric measuring 34 x 28cm (13³/₈ x 11in)
- Sewing thread to match
- Sewing needle
- Small amount of wadding/batting
- Embroidery thread

For the Sheet:
- Fabric measuring 34 x 28cm (13³/₈ x 11in)
- Sewing thread to match
- Sewing needle

For the Pillow:
- Fabric measuring 12 x 16cm (4¾ x 6¼in)
- Sewing thread to match
- Sewing needle
- Small amount of toy stuffing

SIZES
- Mattress: 26 x 15cm (10¼ x 6in)
- Sheet: 24 x 29cm (9½ x 11½in)
- Pillow: 10 x 7cm (4 x 2¾in)

3 Fill gently with a piece of wadding/batting cut to fit inside. Fold a 1cm (³/₈in) seam allowance in along the remaining open edge and press.

4 Sew the seam together by hand using a sewing needle and matching thread. Using a sewing needle and embroidery thread, loop the thread through the mattress and knot. Repeat for each of the six ties.

Top Tip!

If you don't have any wadding/batting you can use toy stuffing instead.

Sheet

1 Fold the fabric over on one long side to make a double seam as follows: fold over by 5mm (¼in) and then fold again by 5mm (¼in) to hide the raw edge.

2 Repeat for the other long side and both short sides. Sew a double seam at either end of the piece of lace, making it the same length as the width of the fabric.

3 Sew the lace in place along the top edge of the fabric.

Pillow

1 Fold the fabric in half with RS together so that your folded piece measures 12 x 8cm (4¾ x 3^1/$_8$in).

2 Using a straight stitch on your sewing machine, sew along one short edge and the long edge leaving a 1cm (^{3}/$_8$in) seam allowance. Turn through and press the seams.

3 Fill gently with a small amount of toy stuffing. Fold a 1cm (^{3}/$_8$in) seam allowance in along the remaining open edge and press.

4 Sew the seam together by hand using a sewing needle and matching thread.

Top Tip!

If you wish to make a special bed for your animal, the bedding will fit nicely inside a small shoe box.

MINI-ME ACCESSORIES

page 135

page 137

page 134

page 136

MOSES BASKET

Instructions

Base

Cast on 6 sts and knit 1 row.
Next row: K1, M1, K to last st, M1, K1 (8 sts).
Knit 1 row.
Repeat last 2 rows twice more (12 sts).
Continue in GS until work measures 9cm (3½in).
Next row: K1, K2tog, K to last 3 sts, K2tog, K1 (10 sts).
Knit 1 row.
Repeat last 2 rows twice more (6 sts).
Cast off.

Top

Cast on 56 sts and knit 10 rows.
Next row: K35, w&t (see page 14).
Next row: K14, w&t.
Next row: K13, w&t.
Next row: K12, w&t.
Next row: K11, w&t.
Next row: K10, w&t.
Next row: Knit to the end of the row.
Knit 1 row.
Cast off.

MATERIALS

- 105m (115yd) DK (8-ply/light worsted) cotton yarn in cream
- Four 10mm buttons
- Matching sewing thread

TOOLS

- 3.25mm (UK 10, US 3) DPN
- Sewing needle

SIZE

- 12cm (4¾in) long and 5cm (2in) high

Handle (make two)

Cast on 4 sts using DPN and work in SS until work measures 2cm (¾in). Work an i-cord (see page 33 under *Ear edging*) until work measures 8cm (3 1/8in), then work in SS in rows until work measures 10cm (4in). Cast off.

Making up

Taking the top of the Moses basket, sew the short side seam. Pin the top to the base, placing the shaped section at one end and using the photograph for guidance. Sew the top to the base.

Pin the handles in place. Taking a button and a sewing needle threaded with matching sewing thread, sew the button through the flat part of the handle to the Moses basket to secure the button and the handle. Repeat for the other three buttons.

SLEEPING BAG

Instructions

> ### Note:
> The sleeping bag is made in one piece.

Cast on 8 sts in MC and knit 4 rows.
Cast on 3 sts at the beginning of the next 2 rows in GS (14 sts).
Knit 1 row.
Join in CC.
Working in CC and starting with a knit row, work 4 rows in SS.
Change to MC and, starting with a knit row, work 2 rows in SS.
Repeat last 6 rows six more times.
Change to CC and work 4 rows in SS.
Change to MC and cut CC as you will now be working only using MC.
Work in GS from here onwards.
Knit 2 rows.
Cast off 3 sts at the beginning of the next two rows (8 sts).
Knit 2 rows.

MATERIALS
- 9m (10yd) of 4-ply (fingering) yarn in pale yellow (MC)
- 9m (10yd) of 4-ply (fingering) yarn in cream (CC)
- Two 8mm buttons

TOOLS
- 3mm (UK 11, US 2/3) knitting needles
- Sewing needle

SIZE
- 6.5cm (2½in) long excluding straps

Next row: K3, cast off 2, K2 (leaving two groups of 3 sts).
Turn and working over these 3 sts only*, continue in GS until strap measures 2cm (¾in).
Next row: K1, YO, K2tog.
Knit 2 rows.
Cast off.*
With WS facing, rejoin yarn to remaining 3 sts and work from * to * once more.

Making up

With RS on the outside, fold the sleeping bag in half and sew the side seams, matching colours. Sew the two buttons in place on the front section of the sleeping bag.

BABY BLANKET

Instructions

Cast on 24 sts and knit 2 rows.
*Next row: K2, (P4, K4) twice, P4, K2.
Next row: K2, (K4, P4) twice, K4, K2.
Repeat last 2 rows twice more.
Next row: K2, (K4, P4) twice, K4, K2.
Next row: K2, (P4, K4) twice, P4, K2.
Repeat last 2 rows twice more*.
Work from * to * once more.
Next row: K2, (P4, K4) twice, P4, K2.
Next row: K2, (K4, P4) twice, K4, K2.
Repeat last 2 rows twice more.
Knit 2 rows.
Cast off.

Making up

Weave in all loose ends in and press lightly.

MATERIALS

- 12m (13yd) of 4-ply (fingering) yarn in pale yellow

TOOLS

- 3mm (UK 11, US 2/3) knitting needles
- Sewing needle

SIZE

- 9.5cm (3¾in) square

BABY SLING

Instructions

Cast on 3 sts and knit 8 rows.
Next row: (K1, M1) twice, K1 (5 sts).
Knit 1 row.
Next row: K1, M1, K3, M1, K1 (7 sts).
Knit 1 row.
Cast on 6 sts at the beginning of the next 2 rows (19 sts).
Knit 6 rows.
Cast off 5 sts at the beginning of the next 2 rows (9 sts).
Next row: K1, ssK, K to last 3 sts, K2tog, K1 (7 sts).
Repeat last row once more (5 sts).
Knit 1 row.
Cut yarn.
Cast on 33 sts, K across 5 sts on needle, cast on 33 sts (71sts).
Knit 1 row
Next row: K2, YO, K2tog, K to last 4 sts, K2tog, YO, K2.
Knit 1 row.
Cast off.

MATERIALS
- 50m (55yd) DK (8-ply/light worsted) cotton yarn in cream
- Two 10mm buttons
- Sewing thread to match

TOOLS
- 3.25mm (UK 10, US 3) knitting needles
- Sewing needle

SIZE
- 6cm (2³/₈in) long

Making up

The cast-on edge forms the bottom of the baby carrier. Using the photograph for guidance, fold the two shorter side pieces to meet in the middle and sew together. Fold the cast-on edge up and sew to this section. This will form the 'seat' of the carrier.

Place the carrier on your animal and bring the straps around the back of the animal to the opposite side of the carrier so that they cross at the back. Mark the position of the two buttons.

Remove the carrier from the animal and sew the buttons securely in place using matching sewing thread and a sewing needle.

TEMPLATES

Fabric Dress Back
Cut 1

Also used for School Dress and Girl's Pyjamas

grain direction

grain direction

Fabric Dress Front
Cut 2 (1 in reverse)

Also used for School Dress

grain direction

Girl's Pyjama Front
Cut 2 (1 in reverse)

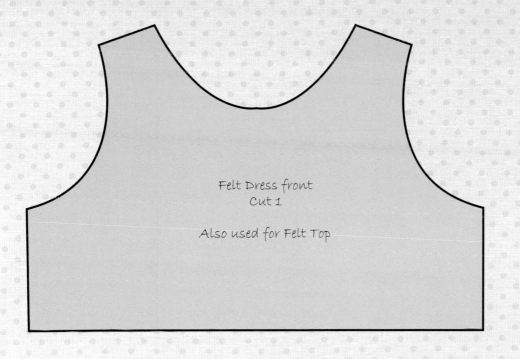

Felt Dress front
Cut 1

Also used for Felt Top

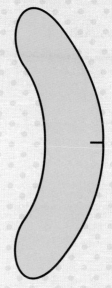

Coat hanger
Cut 1 in brown
cardboard;
Cut 2 in white felt

Felt Dress back
Cut 2
(1 in reverse)

Also used for Felt Top

Heart motif for Felt Dress
Cut 1

Flip flops

Strap Trim
Cut 2

Strap
Cut 1

Sole
Cut 4 in felt and 2 in
heavyweight interfacing

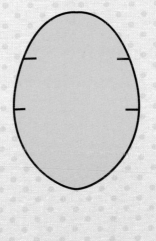

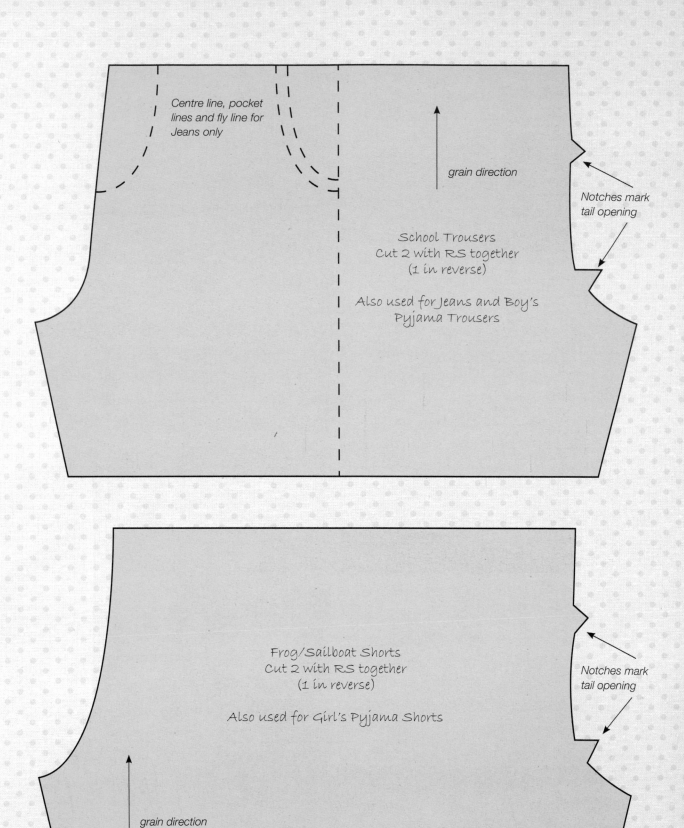

Centre line, pocket
lines and fly line for
Jeans only

grain direction

Notches mark
tail opening

School Trousers
Cut 2 with RS together
(1 in reverse)

Also used for Jeans and Boy's
Pyjama Trousers

Frog/Sailboat Shorts
Cut 2 with RS together
(1 in reverse)

Also used for Girl's Pyjama Shorts

Notches mark
tail opening

grain direction

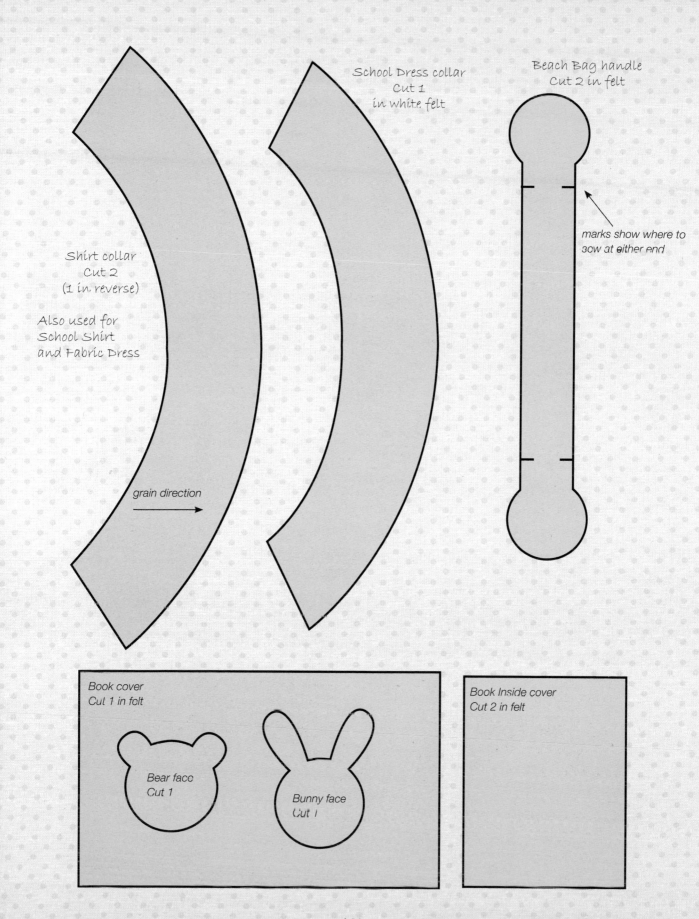

Shirt collar
Cut 2
(1 in reverse)

Also used for
School Shirt
and Fabric Dress

grain direction

School Dress collar
Cut 1
in white felt

Beach Bag handle
Cut 2 in felt

marks show where to
sew at either end

Book cover
Cut 1 in folt

Bear face
Cut 1

Bunny face
Cut 1

Book Inside cover
Cut 2 in felt

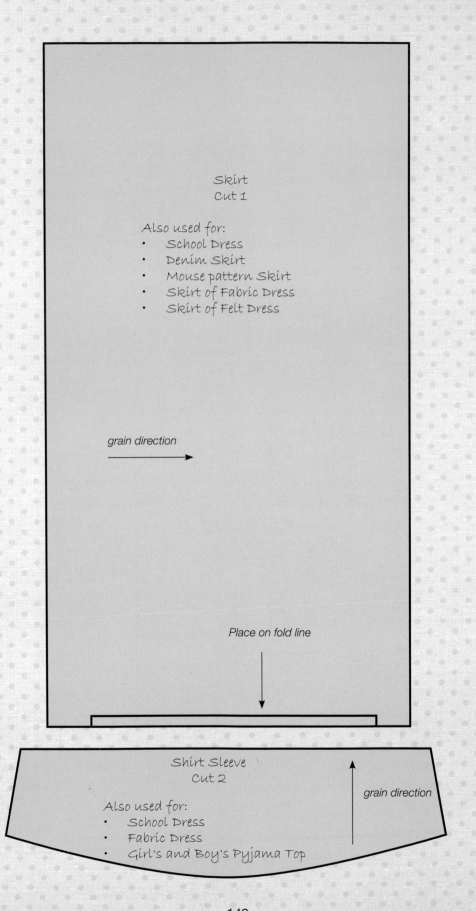

Skirt
Cut 1

Also used for:
- School Dress
- Denim Skirt
- Mouse pattern Skirt
- Skirt of Fabric Dress
- Skirt of Felt Dress

grain direction

Place on fold line

Shirt Sleeve
Cut 2

Also used for:
- School Dress
- Fabric Dress
- Girl's and Boy's Pyjama Top

grain direction

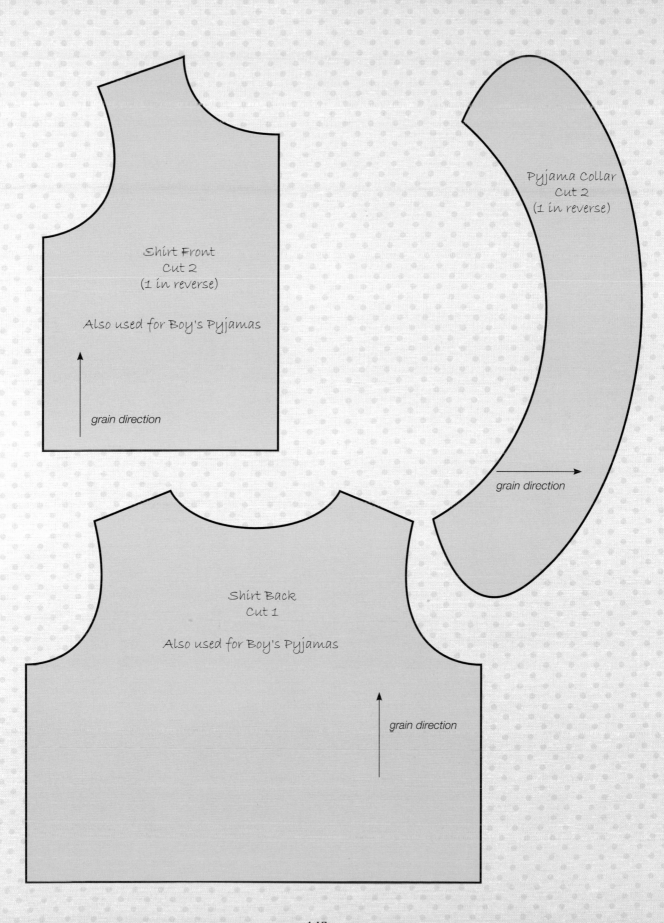

Shirt Front
Cut 2
(1 in reverse)

Also used for Boy's Pyjamas

grain direction

Pyjama Collar
Cut 2
(1 in reverse)

grain direction

Shirt Back
Cut 1

Also used for Boy's Pyjamas

grain direction

INDEX